Co-parenting without Conflict

(A Resource for Practitioners to Support Parents to Minimise Harm to Children)

By

Elaine Nembhard

Copyright Information

Disclaimer:

The author will not accept blame or legal responsibility for any damages or monetary loss due to the information contained within this toolkit. Practitioners are responsible for the way the use the content, therefore must take care to make sure they understand and have the knowledge and skills set to implement the various strategies.

A Practical and Versatile Toolkit for Practitioners

I have used Practitioners to mean anyone working with children and their families – social workers, family support workers, early intervention workers.

We aim to:

- Upskill professionals about parental conflict and how it affects children
- Help Practitioners complete direct work with parents and children
- Design workshops for parents
- Design training courses for staff who are supporting parents in conflict
- Capture and use the child's voice

Contact our Team at Mayday to discuss creating a tailor-made toolkit for your organisation. We offer the following options:

- Co-parenting without conflict (based on this toolkit)
- Complex parenting (*parental alienation, narcissistic parenting, personality disorder)*

- Conflict resolution skills to resolve family conflict (focus on parent-child conflict)

- Domestic violence toolkit (*coercive control, hidden harm, getting the child's voice)*

Training

Mayday Social Work Consultancy and Mayday Domestic Violence Services design and provide training and train the trainer programmes linked to the toolkits.

Evaluating your service or interventions

Alongside our toolkit, we have updated our Logic Model Creator to include Parental Conflict. Originally it focused on child protection concerns, neglect, and abuse to include parental conflict. See our evaluation page or visit https://maydaysocialworkconsultancy.co.uk/logic-model-creator/

CONTENTS

Context

The Government acknowledges that interparental conflict and its negative impact on children are societal problems that need a long-term strategy. There are growing concerns about the financial cost of £46 billion to the taxpayer of family breakdown, including parental conflict and a wide range of services.

In addition to funding provided between 2015- 2018 to increase support for family relationships, the Government announced in 2017 a further 39 million until March 2021 on a national Reducing Parental Conflict (RPC) programme.

The programme aims to tackle destructive inter-parental conflict where parents are in a co-parenting relationship. There is a focus specifically on parental conflict, which is frequent and intense and which parents are unable to resolve satisfactorily.

It draws on evidence-based research highlighting how inter-parental adversely impacts children's mental health and long-term life chances.

The type of conflict that the programme seeks to address is those that do not meet the domestic violence threshold.

The Early Intervention Foundation (EIF) was established in 2013 and commissioned by the Department for Work and Pensions (DWP) to champion and support early intervention work where there are risks to children. It has played a significant role in supporting the RPC's development and their website is a key source of research and planning information.

Acknowledgements

Although I have my name on this toolkit, it has not been a solitary process. Many people have had a hand in helping to bring my ideas to life in this toolkit. The most important contributors have been participants in our training courses and the children and families I worked with as their Social Worker.

Mayday Domestic Violence Services' team has delivered our domestic violence and complex parenting training courses to participants who have shared their experiences and the challenges they face. Their contributions have also helped us to develop and improve our training programmes.

Our team became involved with delivering the RPC programme on behalf of the DWP because we found the RPC training and initiative to be a good fit with what we do.

We are grateful for the research they have carried out and, in particular, their report about 'What works to enhance inter-parental relationships and improve outcomes for children' and all the other information they provided through their collaboration with Professor Gordon Harold from the University of Sussex.

The EIF review into 'What Works....' (by Gordon Harold, Daniel Acquah, Ruth Sellers & Haroon Chowdry) drew some conclusions and recommendations, one of which is:

"Much more needs to be done to test and learn about what works, for whom, and in what circumstances, and about how to implement effective interventions, ensuring the quality of practice, appropriate supervision, and impact. It is important that any future investment from government and other funders builds in effective evaluation and enables commissioners and practitioners working on the ground to share learning."[1]

It gives hope to the idea that further work will be done in the future to reduce parental conflict and improve outcomes for children. We hope that the DWP and commissioners evaluate the effectiveness of their programmes and interventions to inform future developments. We also hope that the training programme will continue and focus on making sure all professionals working together to safeguard children have access to the training.

---

[1] (Gordon, Acquah, Sellers, & Chowdry, 2016)

What I would say is that from our collective experiences, the training programme needs to take into account the different levels of skills that exist across the sector. It needs to focus on interventions for parents such as developing conflict resolution skills.

Finally, I want to thank you for obtaining a copy of this toolkit and hope that you find it useful in supporting the invaluable work you are doing.

We appreciate the work that the DWP has commissioned so far. We also recognise that the RPC programme rollout is in its infancy; therefore, it is difficult to quantify what impact it will have on the parents who are in a co-parenting relationship. More importantly, the effect it will have on children's outcomes.

PART I – Inter-parental Conflict, Concepts and Methods to Resolve Conflict

1. Introduction – About Parental Conflict

Mayday Social Work Consultancy and **Mayday Domestic Violence Services** have been facilitating training courses since 2014 to tackle the growing prevalence of parental conflict from low-level conflict to domestic violence and abuse and parental alienation. Our programmes on teaching conflict resolution skills are aimed at skilling up practitioners to recognise and support parents where there is parental conflict below the threshold of domestic violence. Our focus was to prevent cases escalating to Statutory Children Social Services (SCSS) with this programme.

These cases that do not meet the statutory intervention threshold are increasing the statutory social worker's caseloads. I have first-hand experience working on the frontline of child protection services and holding cases requiring parental conflict interventions rather than SCSS. These cases can significantly increase the number of social workers cases because sometimes there is no other option.

With this in mind, I have created this toolkit to help Practitioners provide early support to parents. My vision is for agencies to provide early support to parents to deal with inter-parental conflict, whether they are living together or apart. It entails Practitioners teaching parents conflict resolution skills either with individual couples or in small workshops. It will include parents who are together or separated but are in a co-parenting relationship.

Safeguarding Concerns

Though the programme is about supporting parents in a co-parenting relationship to deal with intense and frequent conflict occurrences, Practitioners will need to determine whether they are concerned for a child's welfare. If there are safeguarding concerns, it is advisable to refer to Children's Social Services. It might be necessary to have a Child in Need (Section 17, Children Act, 1989) or Child Protection (Section 47, Children Act 1989) plan to protect the children from exposure to further parental conflict.

What do We Mean by Parental Conflict?

The type of parental conflict that we are concerned about is **intense** and **frequent and** causes **damage** to children's wellbeing and life chances. Practitioners need to explore the nature and causes of the conflict. They will need to do so in the context of the couple's relationship, including factors causing stresses and vulnerabilities.

The focus is on the destructive conflict that threatens or can threaten children's positive outcomes and the family's stability.

What happens to the child exposed to destructive parental conflict

A wealth of research findings describes how children from an early age, say six months, are affected by parental conflict. Due to their exposure to their parents' conflict, they can present with health and wellbeing problems in childhood which can have a knock-on effect in their adult life.

Exposure to destructive parental conflict can lead to internalising and externalising behaviours. [2] Some of the behaviours are given below:

Internalising Emotional and psychological state	Externalising Physical state
Depression	Aggression
Anxiety	Hostility
Withdrawn	Anti-social behaviour
Somatic complaints	Non-compliant behaviour

Children face longer-term adverse outcomes when they have been exposed to frequent high-intensity conflict. Areas of outcomes that can be affected include educational, interpersonal, problem-solving, and prosocial skills. The extent of the impact on children will depend on how entrenched or problematic parental conflict has become.

When children experience unresolved conflict between parents, it can store up problems and impact their romantic or intimate relationships. Because of how they were parented, they may grow up using the same parenting strategies their parents used. So, the parental conflict relationship can affect how children deal with their personal relationships and continue into the next generation. [3]

When children witness frequent and intense conflicts between parents, the effects can be traumatising. They can cause long-term problems if

---

[2] (Gordon & Sellers, 2018)
[3] (Asmussen, Fischer, Drayton, & McBride, 2020)

they remain unresolved. If children cannot make sense of what is happening, they may convince themselves that they are the reason for the parental conflict.

Based on their coping strategy, children might internalise their experience and present with problems like anxiety and depression. Very young children might developmentally regress, manifesting in issues like bed-wetting. Adolescent children's problems could see them becoming withdrawn and start self-harming.

Other children might externalise their experience and might act out, exhibiting challenging, aggressive and delinquent behaviours. Some adolescent children can exhibit risky sexual behaviour, alcohol or substance abuse, and be vulnerable to exploitation. These children's lived experiences can create difficulties handling conflicts in their interpersonal relationship, problem-solving, and social life. If the cycle remains unbroken, this can manifest in the same problems repeating itself in adult relationships.

Children respond in different ways to parental conflict

You may have noticed that some of the statements above were not written as absolute facts. The reason is that children's lived experiences affect them in different ways. Two siblings could experience the same high-level parental conflict but have different responses. The impact might be worse for one when compared to the other. Many factors influence this impact, including the child's personality traits, inherent resilience, temperament, age, the children's coping strategies, and the support available to the children, including extended family, school, peers, and other friendships.

Excessive parental conflict can also lead to the neglect or abuse of the children

- Parents who are engaged in excessive conflicts will have their parenting capacity compromised (less energy, time, and focus) to meet their children's needs.

- Parents might take out their anger or frustration on the children.

- Parents might unwittingly share their experience with the children to get them to take sides or to get them to empathise.

- The children might feel confused, helpless, and powerless in this scenario. None of these is healthy for the children.

What Needs to Be Done

The priority must be educating parents about parental conflict which must include a thorough exploration and discussion about the behaviours and triggers leading to conflict. Here are a few:

- Parents who shout and scream at each other, saying hurtful and nasty things to each other.

- The conflict escalates out of control and becomes more and more intense.

- The whole environment becomes tense, unfriendly, uncomfortable for the children.

- It does not take much for arguments to flare-up and gets out of control.

- Awkward silence ensues with demonstrations of possible passive-aggressive behaviour, like silent treatment, avoidance etc. or escalates into violence.

- Issues remain unresolved and get pushed under the carpet, and parents try to be normal however, there is always the inherent danger of conflict.

 Children who witness violence or threats of violence have suffered or, is likely to suffer significant harm and would have experienced trauma. These experiences are child abuse and a safeguarding concern considered abuse that must be reported to the local authority – See the guidance, "Working Together to Safeguard Children" for roles and responsibilities.

Barrier to Practitioners Addressing Parental Conflict

Accessing support is voluntary, and Practitioners have to get parental consent before seeking to support the parents. On this basis, many parents will not take up the offer of support. The Practitioner cannot take any further action unless there are grounds to escalate to SCSC.

Unfortunately, it is not uncommon in SCSS to read the history of a case to see that there had been previous referrals, resulting in offer and refusal of support. Some months or even years down the road, the situation worsens and meets the domestic violence threshold.

2. Identifying the Causes of Parental Conflict

Before we begin to identify the causes, it is essential to distinguish between constructive and destructive conflict. I know from experience working in SCSS that parents sometimes do not accept that conflict between parents is an issue. They will challenge the worker by saying arguing is normal and all couples do it, so they don't see any need for concern. Usually, the reports to SCSS are serious enough to be classified as domestic abuse. In these cases, I would usually stress that yes, it is but the conflict we are talking about but it is at a level that is unacceptable.

I would further explain that experiences of difficulties and conflict in relationships are part of everyday life, and parents usually sort these out without them becoming problematic. When they do, they are showing their children how to resolve conflict.   Children learn from their parents' example and find it easier to resolve disputes with their peers or when they find themselves in conflict situations.

We want parents to understand the type of conflict we are concerned about and why we have these concerns.

The type of parental conflict that we are concerned about is **intense** and **frequent and** causes **damage** to children's wellbeing and life chances. Practitioners need to explore the nature and causes of the conflict. They will need to do so in of the couple's relationship, including factors causing stresses and vulnerabilities.

It is a complicated task influenced by several factors, primarily the parents' insight and willingness to engage with the Practitioner. Begin by considering the context of the conflict.   Parental conflict occurs when there are differences between what the parents want to accomplish, how they approach what they want to achieve, their personal needs, and their expectations of each other's behaviour. [4]

There are many causes of conflict, so exploring the root causes of the conflict is critical to getting the intervention right and avoiding mistakes.

It can be useful to separate potential causes to make it easier to identify them. Here some broad topics concerning actions and behaviours that commonly lead to conflict [5]escalating:

---

[4] (Johnson, 2012)

[5] (Shaw, 2019)

- Miscommunication (the meaning was not communicated in the desired way)
- Lack of information
- Misunderstanding
- Different views or perspectives
- Destructive thought patterns
- Not able to regulate emotions

In family life there many other situations that can lead to or trigger conflict. Some of these that we come across regularly in SCSS are:

- Parental relationship (satisfaction, dissatisfaction)

- Parental response to conflict situation

- Children (matters affecting their children)

- Disagreements on daily household matters

- Situations over which they might not have any control (housing, illness)

- Parental mental health (the range of personality disorders and others)

- Drug and alcohol use (illicit and legal substances)

- Addictive behaviours (gambling, computer gaming, social media, mobile)

- Parental lifestyle (different lifestyles, beliefs and values)

Enduring Vulnerabilities

While some of the causes of conflict are immediately obvious, Practitioners will need to explore the Enduring Vulnerabilities in the relationship or family as they could have implications for ongoing conflict.

Individuals bring pre-existing vulnerabilities to their relationship, thus changing the relationship dynamics over time and contributing to conflict. Karney and Bradbury's 1995[6]) used their Vulnerability Stress Adaptation

---

[6] (Karney & Bradbury, 1995)

Model as a framework for clarifying change in marriages; however, it is relevant to the different couple relationships in our society today[7].

These may take the form of:

- **Personal traits**
  Personality traits reflect people's characteristic patterns of thoughts, feelings, and behaviours.

- **Neuroticism**

  "In psychology and development, a broad personality trait dimension representing the degree to which a person experiences the world as distressing, threatening, and unsafe. Each individual can be positioned somewhere on this personality dimension between extreme poles: perfect emotional stability versus complete emotional chaos.

  Highly neurotic individuals tend to be labile (that is, subject to frequently changing emotions), anxious, tense, and withdrawn. Individuals who are low in neuroticism tend to be content, confident, and stable. The latter report fewer physical and psychological problems and less stress than do highly neurotic individuals."[8]

Similarly, information regarding adverse childhood experiences (ACEs) or family history and functioning can help parents understand, manage or resolve parental conflict.

[9]ACEs are stressful or traumatic events that occur in the first 18 years of a person's life. The more exposed someone is to ACEs, the higher their risk of developing multiple health, social and behavioural problems throughout their life. ACEs can also lead to numerous concurrent health outcomes. For example, childhood abuse can lead to poor self-esteem, resulting in smoking tobacco and drinking alcohol at a young age (contrary to legal requirement) leading to extremely harmful health problems in later life.

Experiencing any ACE can lead to adverse health outcomes and affect brain development and a change in social or emotional behaviour. These changes can lead to making poor choices and adopting risky behaviours that lead to ill-health, disability and even early death.

---

[7] (Gonzaga, Campos, & Bradbury, 2007)
[8] https://www.britannica.com/science/neuroticism
[9] https://www.cdc.gov/violenceprevention/aces/

Parents Responses

How parents respond to conflict can make a difference. Their destructive behaviour in conflicts can manifest in multiple ways and continue unless they develop insight into the issue, create and sustain changes. Parental conflict is an **interpersonal conflict** that occurs where there are disagreements between them because they have different views or incompatible goals.

There are six broad categories of interpersonal conflicts[10] and five responses that people use – see table below:

Category of Conflict

1. **Pseudo conflict** is a conflict due to a perceptual difference between partners and is quickly resolved, an example of which is badgering, light teasing, taunting, and mocking behaviour.

2. **Fact conflict** is a conflict due to a dispute over the truth or accuracy of a piece of information.

3. *Value* **conflict** is a conflict due to disagreements about deep-seated moral beliefs.

4. **Policy conflict** is the conflict that is due to a disagreement over a plan or course of action.

5. **Ego conflict** is the conflict due to both parties in a disagreement insisting on being the "winner" of the argument.

6. **Meta conflict** is a conflict due to disagreements about the process of communication itself during an argument.

The conflict between parents falls into more than one of these categories as parents have interpersonal differences, disagree on many issues but take steps to resolve these quickly and amicably. The problem escalates where parents cannot resolve their differences regardless of the category it falls into, and it then becomes destructive and harmful to children.

---

[10] https://www.healthline.com/health/interpersonal-conflict & conflict-types

The following are possible responses to the conflict, and what parents chose to do will determine what happens next.

Conflict Responses

1. **Withdrawing** is resolving a conflict by physically or psychologically removing oneself from the conflict.

2. *Accommodating* is resolving conflict by satisfying the other person's needs or accepting others' ideas while neglecting one's own needs or ideas.

3. *Forcing* is resolving a conflict by satisfying one's own needs. It involves advancing your ideas of the other person or for the relationship.

4. *Compromising* is resolving conflict by mutually agreeing with one's partner to satisfy each other's needs or interests partially.

5. *Collaborating* is resolving a conflict by using problem-solving to arrive at a solution that meets both needs and interests of the parties involved in the conflict.

3. Destructive Conflict Behaviours

Parents sometimes do not recognise when they are engaging in any destructive conflict behaviours. Therefore, it is up to the Practitioner to explore how parents respond to each other and identify patterns.

You are looking for behaviours that fall into these categories:

Destructive Conflict Behaviours

1. **Constant arguing**, is a conflict pattern in which the parents argue about the same issue over and over.

2. **Counter-blaming** is behaviour in which one moves the focus of the argument away from oneself by blaming the other person.

3. **Cross-complaining** is a conflict pattern in which partners trade unrelated criticisms, leaving the initial issue unresolved.

4. **Demand-withdrawal** is a pattern of behaviour in which one partner consistently demands while the other person withdraws.

5. **Mutual hostility** is a conflict pattern in which partners trade increasingly louder verbal abuse, including inappropriate, unrelated personal criticism, name calling, swearing, and sarcasm.

Examples of Destructive and Constructive Conflict Behaviours

Relationship experts like Dr. John Gottman describes four destructive conflict behaviours that damage intimate relationships. He used the biblical metaphor, **the four horsemen of the apocalypse**[11] , to illustrate the message. If left unresolved, these four issues will cause permanent damage to the relationship.

---

[11] Ellie Lisitsa (2013), The Gottman Institute

The Four Horsemen Explained

Criticism: being critical of the other person and verbally attacking personality or character

Contempt: Being scornful towards the other person, attacking the person's sense of self or identity with the intention to abuse or insult.

Defensiveness: victimising yourself to stop a perceived attach and reverse the blame.

Stonewalling: Withdrawing to avoid conflict and convey disapproval, distance, and separation.

Note: We will address how you can support parents to counteract these damaging behaviours later on in the toolkit.

Parental Behaviours

As previously mentioned, it is vital to understand whether the parents' behaviour meets the threshold for domestic abuse. In some cases, it will, due to the children's exposure to frightening, harmful behaviours.

Examples of behaviours in conflict situations:

- Arguing at home and in public)
- Raised voices
- Physical actions/ behaviours (e.g., 'storming' out, smashing objects, breaking down doors)
- Silences/stonewalling
- Using disrespectful language
- Non-stop bickering/snapping
- Resentment or anger presented through body language
- Showing open annoyance
- On-going criticism of partner

- Different views on parenting
- Mood swings or mood changes
- Arguing using smartphones (texting and social media)

Impact on Relationship

Parental conflict behaviours are a serious concern that can irrevocably damage the parental relationship and adversely impact their children. Children are often the biggest losers when there are conflict and possible parental separation.

Understanding the conflict situation, accepting their role in it, and being motivated to change are crucial steps to making progress.

4. Factors to Consider When Assessing Parental Conflict

Before starting work with families, to be effective, Practitioners must consider their approach to what they are seeking to achieve and how they go about it. Equally important is a good understanding of the context in which the Practitioner is working. The following is not a definitive list of the practice issues that needs to be taken into account, but they are key to understanding and working with families.

Different Types of Family Structures

Family structures have evolved over the years resulting in different types of family set-up, some of which are considered below:

Nuclear Family

The nuclear family is the traditional type of family structure. This family type consists of two parents and children. The nuclear family was long held in esteem by society as the ideal for raising children. Children in nuclear families receive strength and stability from the two-parent structure and generally have more opportunities accorded by the financial security provided by adults.

Extended Family

The extended family structure consists of two or more adults related, either by blood or marriage, living in the same home. This family includes many relatives residing together and working toward mutual goals, such as raising the children and keeping up with household chores. Many extended families have cousins, aunts or uncles, and grandparents living together. This type of family structure may develop due to financial challenges or because older relatives cannot fully care for themselves.

Step Family or Blended Family

A stepfamily, blended family, bonus family, or instant-family is a family where at least one parent has children that are not biologically or adoptive related to the other spouse or partner. Either parent or both may have children from previous relationships.

Regardless of whether couples are married or co-habiting, separation is common in families. The situation leads to the creation of blended or stepfamilies as two separate families merging into one new unit. It consists of a new husband, wife, partner, and children from previous marriages or relationships.

Same-sex

Same-sex or civil partner couples with children are becoming more common in the UK. The family structure can be complex, and practitioners will need to identify the co-parenting arrangements in place.

Same-sex attracted people create families through a mixture of different conception methods processing, fostering, and adoption. Some examples arrangements of same-sex parented families are:

- a single lesbian who has children from a previous heterosexual relationship;
- a co-parenting arrangement between a lesbian couple and a gay male couple;
- a gay male couple having children through surrogacy; and a
- bisexual man having children with a heterosexual woman.

Grandparent Family

For a variety of reasons, nowadays, many grandparents are raising their grandchildren. Indeed, many Children Social Work Services depend on grandparents to care for their grandchildren when their parents cannot do so themselves. The length of time[12] may vary from short-term to long-term, and the conditions may be informal or formal Court Orders. There are families where the parents are not present in the child's life, so grandparents are technically their parents.

Single Parent Family

The single-parent family consists of one parent raising one or more children on his or her own. This family may include a single mother with her children, a single dad with his kids, or a single person. The single-parent family is the most significant change society has seen in terms of family structure changes.

[13]According to the Office for National Statistics (ONS), in 2019, there were 2.9 million lone-parent families in the UK. The report states that this number had not changed much since 2008, when there were 2.8 million single-parent households. What is not clear is how many of these are recorded as single-parent even though they co-parent their children.

---

[12] https://www.mja.com.au/journal/2013/199/2/what-makes-same-sex-parented-family
[13] Office for National Statistics, 2019

Some challenges faced by parents in family structures

All families are different and should be treated as unique despite their similarities and the problems presented. There is no **right** or **wrong answer for** which family structure might experience conflict the most.

There will be a range of relevant issues to the families, and therefore it is important to consider diversity and difference when working with families. When it comes to relationships and stressors, many of the challenges will be the same. However, there might be additional stressors for families due to their difference, for example, ethnicity, disability, and sexuality. Same-sex parents might face additional challenges regarding being accepted into society and feel supported.

*Over and over, **Serious Case Reviews (SCRs)** highlight the need for practitioners to be alert to the risk of **fixed thinking and perceptual bias**. Professor Eileen Munro's report (2005), drew attention to the reoccurrences in SCRs about the great lengths abusive parents will go to deceive practitioners.*

Practitioners also need to be alert to prejudice and discrimination and address these when working with parents.

Bias Awareness

Differences between the family and the Practitioner's backgrounds can lead to bias and assumptions, so Practitioners must always be attentive to their behaviour, thinking, and decision making.

The issue of bias is very complex, and Practitioners are encouraged to develop their knowledge and practices on the subject. Briefly, **bias** is a prejudice in favour of or against one thing, person, or group compared with another, usually in a way that's considered unfair. Biases may be held by an individual, group, or institution and can have negative or positive consequences.

More than anything, this short section is concerned with perception bias which is the tendency to form simplistic stereotypical views and make assumptions about certain groups of people. This leads to judgements being made about parents of diverse groups, which are not objective and is therefore unfair and sometimes discriminatory.

Wake Up - Overcoming Biases

To be able to challenge personal biases, you must be aware of them. Doing this entails a process of reverse engineering, where you look at a statement you hold to be "true" and work your way backwards through deep-rooted assumptions, interpretations, and cognitive bias.

To get you started, here are three relevant examples:

Privilege - be aware that as a Practitioner or professional working with families, you may have experienced more "privilege" growing up than the families you support. How has your "privilege" impacted how you work with families?

Culture – question whether cultural differences between you and the family affects how you view the presenting issue. Spend time checking and reflecting on your experiences of working with or talking to families from different cultures.

Teen parents – how do you approach your work with teen parents; is it different from working with older parents?

Always FACT-CHECK your Assumptions

Sometimes when we **THINK**, we base our assumptions and interpretation on "facts" in reality, we are basing them on assumptions. That is where we get ourselves entangled and confused. Trusting faulty logic is how we make bad choices and cause misunderstanding between people.

- Do not overlook the external cases of others' behaviour.

- Identify your stereotypes

- Evaluate people based on objective factors

- Avoid making rash decisions

Equality Legislation

Differences can be significant and have implications for the quality and effectiveness of the intervention offered to parents.   In assessing their needs, the Practitioner needs to go beyond the legal duties under the Equality Act, 2010, which makes it against the law to discriminate against someone because of a protected characteristic.

As a reminder, overleaf are the nine protected characteristics that have protection from discrimination:

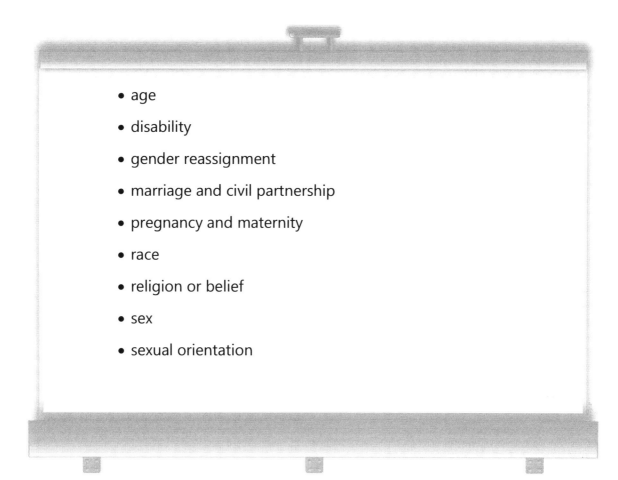

- age

- disability

- gender reassignment

- marriage and civil partnership

- pregnancy and maternity

- race

- religion or belief

- sex

- sexual orientation

When thinking about going beyond the legal duties outlined in the Equality Act, 2010, which most Practitioners will be aware of, you may want to consider using the framework below to guide your practice.

THE G.R.A.C.E.S

Using the **'G.R.A.C.E. S** framework (see below) is a step in the right direction. The concept developed by John Burnham, 1993[14] can help Practitioners to consider the visible and invisible aspects of the parents to identify and explore factors that might impact their lives and behaviours. Its flexibility allows for expansion. For example, Adverse Childhood Experiences (ACEs).

In addition to the usual framework, you can add others such as Adverse Childhood Experiences (ACES). If appropriate, the Practitioner can add to this framework when working with families.

---

[14] The concept was developed by John Burnham in 1993

G: Gender, Gender Identity, Geography, Generation

R: Race, Religion

A: Age, Ability, Appearance. Adverse Childhood Experiences

C: Class, Culture, Caste

E: Education, Ethnicity, Economic Status

S: Spirituality, Sexuality, Sexual Orientation

5. Assessing and Understanding Parents' Needs

You may or may not be fully conversant with formal needs assessment and support planning process. As a reminder, the process involves:

Gathering information: Gathering information about what is happening, including current stressors and enduring vulnerabilities.

Gathering information must include the voice of each child.

Exploring options Use the assessment information and views to planning **the intervention** or support

Agreeing on a plan Agree on the plan with the parents

Implementing the plan Implement or start the support, build rapport to gain a greater understanding of the presenting issues.

Reviewing Continually review progress and the effectiveness of the support being offered. Is it fit for purpose and has the parental conflict reduced?

Parents often deal with multiple on-going difficulties in their lives and view these as a part of everyday life. Because parents deal with problems that they see as part of everyday life, they may not recognise that what they are dealing with is causing parental conflict. Consequently, they remain unaware of the negative impact on their children and their relationship. Focusing on dealing with multiple problems can lead to parents not prioritising their children's emotional health needs and the parental relationship.

As the parental relationship's strength is crucial to achieving positive outcomes for children, parents must be encouraged to prioritise support for the parental relationship.

Parents need to understand what parental conflict is about, the triggers and, behaviours associated with conflict situations. The conversation needs to focus on the negative impact on their children and the necessity to change.

Improving parents' understanding will help with teaching them how to manage or resolve their conflict. They need to understand it is about the conflict between parents of domestic abuse.

To ensure parents understand, Practitioners themselves need to have legal knowledge and understanding of **domestic abuse**. They will need to differentiate between parental conflict and domestic abuse and action they need to take where domestic abuse is a factor.

If you are not sure what the differences are, now might be a good time to reflect and consider the question entirely. For this purpose, see the table below to help with your reflection.

Parental Conflict	V	Domestic Abuse or (Violence)

If you are unfamiliar with what to consider when differentiating between inter-parental conflict and domestic abuse, you might help to use the [15]Duluth Model of Power and Control. Also, consider the legal perspective defined by the Crown Prosecution Service (CPS).

---

[15] https://www.theduluthmodel.org/wheels

Use the following tool to guide your understanding of what is happening within the parents' relationship and how this might be affecting the children.

Healthy

- Open and honest communication
- Mutual respect
- Trust and confidence in each other
- Make important decisions together
- Support each other

Inter-parental conflict

- Disagreements happens often and are intense
- Frequent fights (non-violent)
- Difficulties are minimised, not recognised or addressed
- Non-communicative
- Lack of open & honest communication
- Boundaries are not respected
- Situational couple conflict, abuse, violence both ways

Abusive

- Day to day unresolved and unresolvable conflicts; no consistent pattern of 'victim' or 'abuser'
- Controlling/ abusive behaviour. Coercive control and physical harm
- One partner fears the other

Children are experiencing constructive resolution of any arguments, characterised by mutual respect and emotional control

Children beginning to be affected by conflict between their parents

Children being significantly adversely affected; children's mental health and/or behaviour being affected.

Children at risk of significant harm; children being traumatised

Adapted by Elaine Nembhard (original idea from the Intimate Relationship Spectrum)[16]

---

[16] Stefanou Foundation

Please be aware that this is not a definitive exercise to determine whether the threshold for domestic abuse has been met. Practitioners must follow the threshold guidance from the local authority where they work.

Parents' Needs:

Your approach to the assessment must explore the wide range of issues contributing to the ongoing conflict. When assessing the parents' needs, there will be many things to consider as the situation might be more complex than first thought.

Remember, parents might not recognise what is happening in their relationship and that it is causing conflict.

Below is a 'crib sheet' that can help as a reminder of what to look for and identify the presenting problem and associated behaviours:

Potential Causes Conflict in Relationships

- Relationship breakdown

- Commitment to a partner

- Infidelity (including online)

- Unplanned pregnancies

- Lack of experience with relationships

- Non-compliance with child contact arrangements

- Non-compliance with child maintenance arrangements

- Different expectations of the relationship

- Living arrangements

- Low partner support

- Possessive/Controlling behaviours

- Financial abuse

- Arguing and verbal abuse

- Addictive behaviours (pornography, gambling and computer gaming)

- Addictive behaviours (drugs and alcohol)

- Different parenting styles

- Low parental involvement

- Different parenting styles

- Low family involvement

- Values and Cultural differences

Other Issues Can Cause Parental Conflict

- Money including debts
- Unemployment or work issues
- Housing
- Friends
- Close and wider family relationships
- Household chores
- Social Media
- Sex and intimacy
- Roles in the relationship
- Sex and intimacy
- Children including behaviours
- Gaming (gambling or playing computer games)

The next step in the assessment process is to analyse the information to learn more about the problem so that the planning stage can be completed.

Children's Difficulties and Parental Conflict

[17]Some situations will put stress on the parents' relationship that might relate to their children. It is important to consider these situations and ensure there is support for the children and their parents:

- A child with challenging behaviours
- A child with developmental disorders (e.g., *attention deficit hyperactivity disorder (ADHD), cognitive difficulties*)
- Mental health difficulties
- Physical health difficulties
- Learning difficulties

When children are presenting with behavioural difficulties, it is vital to explore how they affect them. Don't simply attribute a child's challenging behaviour to the child being difficult. We know from research that parental conflict can adversely impact in many ways.

The issues identified below and overleaf are examples and is not an exhaustive list:

- Withdrawn, introverted
- Anxiety, low mood and depression
- Exhibiting violent or intimidating behaviours (in school, towards peers, parents and siblings)
- Showing concern and empathy for a distressed parent
- Displaying signs of emotional distress - crying a lot, being 'clingy' (younger children)
- Becoming argumentative (frequently young teenagers)
- Exhibiting disruptive behaviours – criticising parents, silences, disappearing to bedrooms, confronting parents
- School - (unable concentrate, poor achievement and attendance)
- Playing one parent off against the other
- Unsettled sleep patterns and bedwetting (younger children)

---

[17] (Gordon, Acquah, Sellers, & Chowdry, 2016)

Children's Needs - Applying Maslow's Hierarchy of Needs

When assessing parent's and children's needs, Maslow's Hierarchy of Needs is a good place to start. There is also the Framework for Assessing Children in Need and their Families, which is used throughout SCSS and discussed after this section.

Children spend a significant number of hours daily in the care of early childcare and education professionals. However, unless something appears troubling or seriously wrong, professionals tend not to think too deeply about their life at home. When they misbehave, there is a tendency to blame it on a child's natural behaviour rather than think systematically about their family life and their lived experiences outside these establishments and how those factors may influence their responses. In this instance, we are concerned about how parental conflict impacts children's emotional wellbeing, behavioural health, and outcomes.

This section of the toolkit, together with getting the child's voice, seeks to convey to Practitioners how they can successfully support children and optimise positive outcomes. Practitioners can use 'Maslow's Hierarchy of Needs' to identify and assist with children's developmental needs.

[18]Abraham Maslow developed his psychological theory in 1943 and argued that human beings have several levels of needs. These needs are displayed in the form of a pyramid, as in the diagram below. On the first rung of the pyramid are basic human needs (food, water, clothing, etc.), and at the top is self-actualization (the finding of purpose).

Each need builds upon the level below it, e.g., for children's safety and security needs to be met, they must first have their basic human needs met. Once basic human needs are met, the next step of the pyramid (relationship) needs to be completed until self-actualization is reached.

Applying the Hierarchy to children

Practitioners need a thorough understanding of Maslow's Hierarchy of needs because it presents a more comprehensive context to relate to a child's behaviours and actions. It is common to view children's behaviour in isolation rather than as a part of their more comprehensive lived experiences.

---

[18] (Maslow, 1987)

Asking focused questions regularly to elicit if a child's basic needs are being met should help Practitioners consider whether there may be other reasons for a child's behaviour. When more immediate needs are not met, such as one's needs for food and safety, it becomes increasingly unlikely that a child will be able to behave, learn, and listen to the best of their ability.

Overview of each of Maslow's Needs:

[19]Disruptions due to parental conflict can lead to children having their needs met.

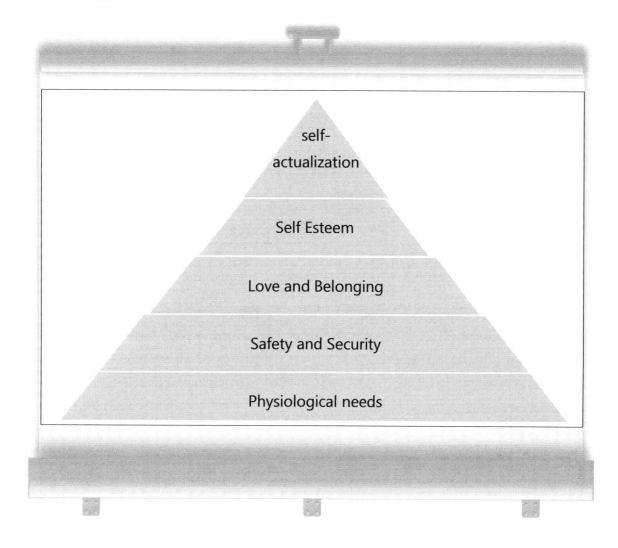

Physiological needs (basic human needs):

These needs are at the core of what is needed to function as a human being. They are essential to our survival. They include but are not limited to:

- Breathing, food, water, shelter, sleep, and clothing.

---

[19] (Maslow, A theory of human motivation, 1943)

Safety and Security:

To thrive and live healthy lives, children (all humans beings) need a sense of safety and security. Children's sense of safety and security needs consistency and predictability, with age-appropriate routines in a comfortable environment.

Love and Belonging (Healthy Relationships):

A healthy relationship with a caring adult is an essential factor in children's development journey. Healthy relationships are relationships that are emotionally, physically, psychologically appropriate.

Self Esteem:

Self-esteem needs include confidence, strength, self-belief, personal and social acceptance. Having these needs met means having a better chance of reaching self-actualization.

Children need to achieve just as much as adults do, and they have the right to do this in line with age-related development. Achieving may relate to education, social or personal development, all of which can be negatively affected by their lived experiences.

Self-Actualization:

When discussing self-actualization concerning children, reflect the child's ability to be creative, be self-confident, act without fear, and find purpose at that stage of their life.

Using the Framework for Assessing Children in Need and their Families [20]

Assessing a child's need and the nature of these needs requires a systematic approach for gathering and analysing information about all children and their families. The Framework guidance is underpinned by legislation, extensive research and practice knowledge outlined in the practice guidance.

Though the focus is on the parents' capacity to meet the child's needs, it is similar to those needs presented in Maslow's Hierarchy of needs. The

---

[20] (Department of Health, 2001)

question is whether parental conflict impacts the parents' capacity to meet the child's needs outlined in the Framework:

Basic Care

Providing for the child's physical needs and appropriate medical and dental care. Also included are food, drink, warmth, shelter, clean and proper clothing and adequate personal hygiene.

Ensuring Safety

Ensuring the child is adequately protected from harm or danger. Included are:

- protection from significant harm or danger, and contact with unsafe adults/other children and from self-harm. Recognition of hazards and risk both in the home and elsewhere.

Emotional Warmth

Ensuring the child's emotional needs are met and giving the child a sense of being specially valued and a positive sense of own racial and cultural identity. Emotional warmth includes ensuring the child's requirements for secure, stable and affectionate relationships with significant adults, appropriate sensitivity and responsiveness to their needs. Appropriate physical contact, comfort and cuddling sufficient to demonstrate warm regard, praise and encouragement.

Stimulation

The child's learning and intellectual development is promoted through encouragement and cognitive stimulation and promoting social opportunities. It includes facilitating the child's cognitive development and potential through interaction, communication, talking and responding to the child's language and questions, encouraging and joining the child's play, and promoting educational opportunities. Enabling the child to experience success and ensuring school attendance to access opportunities. Facilitating child to meet challenges of life.

Guidance and Boundaries

The child is supported to regulate their own emotions and behaviour. The key parental tasks are demonstrating and modelling appropriate behaviour and control of emotions and interactions with others, and guidance. It involves setting boundaries so that the child can develop an internal model of moral values, conscience and social behaviour appropriate for the society within which they will grow up.

The aim is to enable the child to grow into an autonomous adult, hold personal values, and demonstrate appropriate behaviour with others rather than depend on rules outside themselves. It includes social problem solving, anger management, consideration for others, and effective discipline and behaviour shaping.

Stability

The provision of a sufficiently stable family environment enables a child to develop and maintain a secure attachment to the primary caregiver(s) to ensure optimal development. It includes: ensuring secure attachments are not disrupted, providing consistency of emotional warmth over time and responding similarly to the same behaviour. Parental responses change and develop according to the child's developmental progress. Also, ensuring children keep in contact with important family members and significant others.

Note: All of the domain above can be negatively affected by inter-parental conflict.

Strength-Based Thinking and Approach in Assessment

Supporters of a strengths approach believe that anything that assists an individual in dealing with life's challenges is a strength. As mentioned before, parents are not a homogenous group, so it would be challenging to draw up an exhaustive checklist of strengths to consider during the assessment phase. Social workers working in safeguarding services will have ideas of the strengths they think worth considering because it keeps the children safe.

Many assessment tools tend to focus on deficits and inadequacies, so Practitioners should take personal responsibility for ensuring they also incorporate strength factors.

Practitioners could look to the ROPES: Resources, Opportunities, Possibilities, Exceptions, and Solutions[21] (Graybeal, 2001) model to

---

[21] (Graybeal, 2001)

guide strength-based assessments as it was developed for this purpose.

Using frameworks focused on strengths and weaknesses encourages a holistic and balanced assessment of an individual's strengths and problems within a specific situation. Strength-based thinking can help Practitioners to discover the parents' greatest qualities including:

- Personal qualities

- Positive experiences

- Individual initiative

- Personal responsibility

- Capacity to act

- Relationships

- Passion and interests

- NOTES -

Part II –Tools and Ideas to Carry Out Assessments Before Intervening

Note:

The tools in this section are varied, and the Practitioner will need to select the tool that they and the parents feel will work best. The tools are versatile and do not always need the Practitioner to be involved as parents can use them to self-assess.

About the Tools in the Section

This section includes some **tools** that you might find useful in gathering information and assessing parent's and children's needs.

It might seem to be a simple statement, but it is essential to know everything about the problem you are trying to deal with so, the first thing to do is to explore the problem and the presenting issues.

When assessing parental or family needs, Practitioners must keep in mind that children, parents, and families are not a homogenous group. Society consists of parents who are cohabiting, separating, separated or divorced, and in same- or opposite-sex relationships.

List of Tools

Impact of Parent's Vulnerabilities, History, and Functioning

Conflict Escalation - Up and down the Escalator

Approaches to Conflict Resolution

Parents' Understanding of What is Required to Change

How Do Parents Respond to Conflict – Questionnaire

How Do Parents Respond to Conflict – Cards

Relationship Scaling Tool

A Road Map to Damaging Relationships

Relationship Stages

Relationship Scaling (Distressed to Harmony)

Relationship See-Saw

Relationship Wheel

What are some signs of a relationship in distress

Vulnerability Stress Adaptation (VSA)

6.1 Understanding Parents' Vulnerabilities, History and Functioning, and Its Impact

Consider the risk factors that could be contributing to conflict and could potentially lead to children experiencing ACEs. Risk factors for ACEs include:

- Physical, emotional, sexual abuse and neglect

- Mental illnesses

- Imprisonment

- Domestic abuse/intimate partner violence

- Substance abuse

- Divorce or separation

- Poverty

- Homelessness

These are all relevant to enduring vulnerabilities that can contribute to parental conflict.

Though the above list is not an exhaustive one, and Practitioners will need to treat each case as unique as there might be other things that could be contributing to their enduring vulnerabilities. You might want to consider the areas of social G.R.A.C.E.S to ensure a holistic approach.

The quality of the parental relationship is a protective factor for children therefore this area has significance. Though there may be enduring vulnerabilities and stressors, there may be sufficient protective factors or experiences that will help the parents deal with these events and mitigate the development of ACES. Protective factors may include but not limited to:

- A healthy relationship with parents

- Supportive and safe social environment

- Support from professionals, families, and communities where individuals live and interact

- Help in identifying and cultivating a sense of purpose

- Stable housing environment

- Educational opportunities

- Socioeconomic advantages

Tips for Parents to Increase Protective Behaviours

Avoid the following:

- arguing in front of your children

- asking your children to carry hostile messages to your partner

- asking your children upsetting questions about your partner

- asking your children to hide information

- making your children feel like they have to hide positive feelings about each of you from the other

- criticising your partner in front of your children.

It's also important to **let children know that they are not the problem**. You can do this by:

- making sure children understand that the argument isn't about them – it's between you and your partner

- telling your children that you are working on a solution to the problem

- reminding yourself that some problems are for adults to sort out – children don't always need to know what the problem is, and it's OK not to tell them.

Vulnerability Stress Adaptation (VSA) Tool

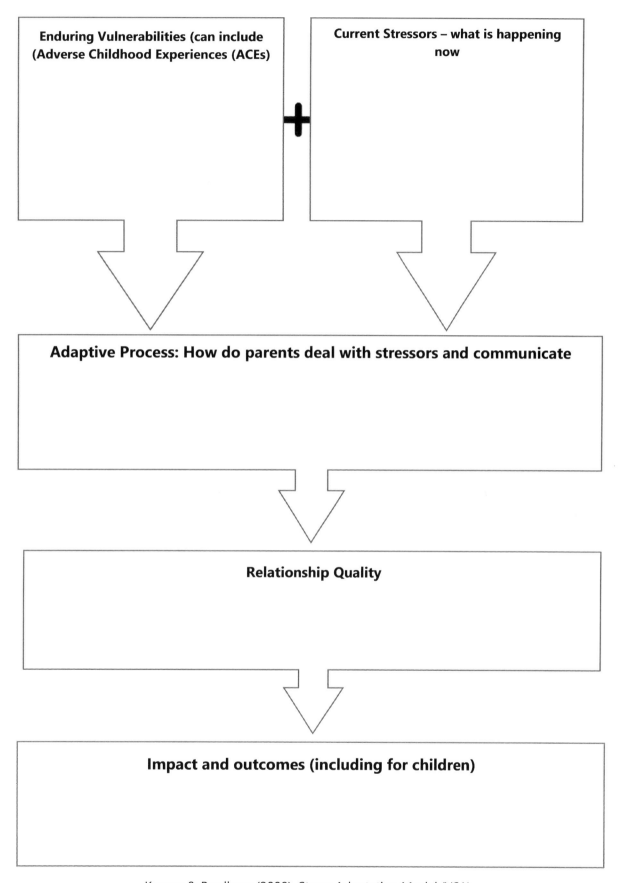

Karney & Bradbury (2000), Stress Adaptation Model (VSA)

6.2 Conflict Escalation - Up and Down the Escalator

Practitioners can use the different outcomes outlined to demonstrate to parents how the conflict in their relationship can get out of control.

Remember, using different techniques and resources to communicate the message is critical because you will come across diversity in the way people learn and respond to these. Using the conflict escalator is another way of showing how conflict escalates and the implications.

[22] **Frederick Glasl's Model of Conflict Escalation**

---

[22] Based on Frederick Glasl's Model of Conflict Escalation

The escalation model uses a traffic light system as follows:

Green: there is every chance that things can be resolved and usually are

Amber: things are getting worse but can still be resolved albeit, doing so need working on

Red: There is no chance of resolving things amicably and everything chance that things will end badly

Approaches to Conflict Resolution

How things turn out will depend on how those involved respond, and clearly, a constructive response is the best way forward

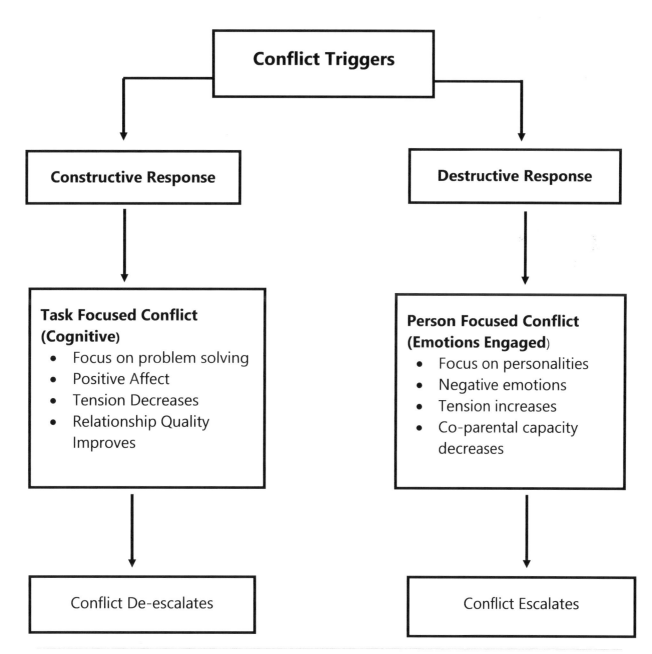

6.3 Parents' Understanding of What is Required to Change

Thomas-Kilmann, 1974 Model[23] can be used to highlight different ways individuals try to resolve conflict. Explaining to parents what results they will get from their position can help them see why they need to change tactics.

Anything other than Win-Win is likely to have some harmful consequences for their children. Being able to resolve conflict to get a Win-Win position is expected to positively impact children as parents are role modelling how to resolve disputes successfully.

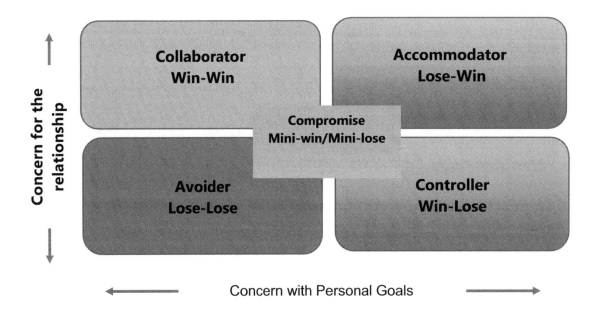

The Thomas-Kilmann Model of Conflict Management Styles

Collaborator = Win-Win

Win-Win is about a cooperative attitude as parents want to resolve the conflict or their problem. Parents are assertive and collaborative and can evaluate their different views. It involves listening and understanding the other person's position, their needs and usually leads to productive and meaningful ways of resolving conflict.

---

[23] (Thomas & Kilmann, 2008)

40

Accommodator = Lose-Win

Lose-Win is the style involving one parent being deeply concerned for others and less concerned for themself. In a conflict situation, this parent will demonstrate a strong desire to maintain peace and consequently dreads conflict. They will work hard to smooth things over, keep the peace, and readily give in, but it does not resolve anything.

It has the potential to lead to conflict as one person is not having their needs met.

Controller = Win-Lose

A Win-Lose situation can contribute to intense parental conflict. It is usually underpinned by competition and the need for one parent to win. The competitive parent is only concerned for themselves, so children in this situation might not be at the forefront of their consideration. A parent preoccupied with winning an argument may be predisposed to use harmful tactics to win. Their main aim is to get their own needs met, and they will use power and control tactics to achieve their objective. At some point, they may resort to aggressive and uncooperative behaviours, use threats, deceit, and manipulation.

Avoider = Lose-Lose

The Lose-Lose situation style of dealing with conflict is not to do anything. In this situation, one parent will be more concerned about others, especially the other parent, than about themselves.

The avoider refused to face the issues and often will not provide direct answers about the conflict.

People who use this style tend to blame themselves, make concessions early, and find it hard to say no.[24]

Compromise = Mini-win/Mini-lose

The position taken in this situation is middle of the road, give and take by both partners, but they seldom confront the conflict.

Consequently, it can deteriorate over time leading to dissatisfaction and the conflict becoming intense and frequent.

---

[24] (Warschaw , 1980)

6.4 Parents' Readiness to Change

Practitioners must make sure **both parents** are at the same stage on the **cycle of change** (see fig 3) before starting the conflict resolution intervention.   It might prove difficult sometimes, and parents might have a different perspective on what is happening and the need to change.

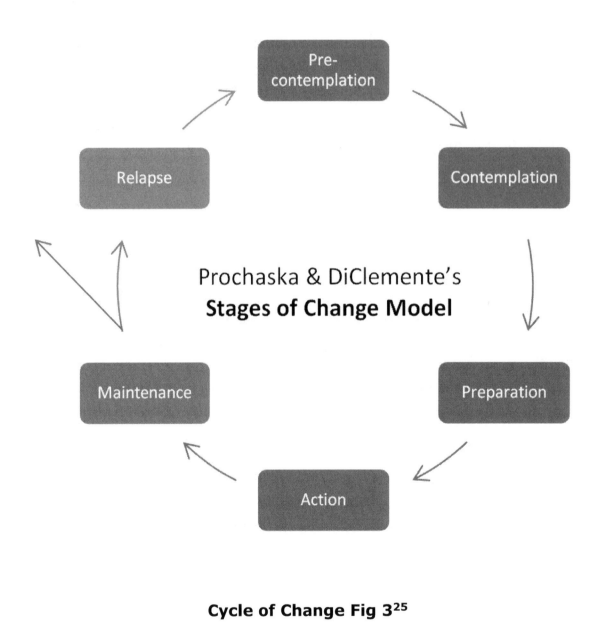

Cycle of Change Fig 3[25]

[25] Prochaska and DiClemente, 1982 and Morrison, 2010

Readiness to Change Ruler

The diagram of a "Ruler" for this exercise is on following pages. It is more user-friendly for working directly with parents. It is simple and effective in assessing readiness and motivation to change. The "Ruler" uses a scale of **1 to 10 t**o gauge parents' readiness to change – again, both parents must be at the same stage.

When assessing whether parents will make **changes**, you will need to be confident that individuals have what it takes:

- Capacity
- Opportunity
- Motivation

If you have had motivational interviewing training, you can use 'change talk' at each stage to move parents along the Ruler.

To successfully navigate the hurdles of Motivational Interviewing, you need to recognise change talk when it occurs.

In the world of Motivational Interviewing, the acronym **DARN CAT**[26] is used as a mnemonic to describe various types of change talk:

- **D**esire
- **A**bility
- **R**easons
- **N**eeds
- **C**ommitment language
- **A**ction (current movement)
- **T**aking steps toward change

---

[26] (Resnicow, Gobat, & Naar, 2015)

Pre-contemplation - one or both parents is not interested In change and is stuck at this stage. Lack of understanding or insight into concerns about parental conflict and the impact on their children.

Next step:

Parents need to understand what parental conflict is, the concern about their behaviour, and show increased interest in changing their behaviour.

Tips:

- Don't force parents to engage in behavioural change if they are not ready, as this could lead to false or disguised compliance.

- Make sure that parents know that making changes is their choice.

- You might ask, "what it might take to move from their current stage of the Ruler?"

- Close the session with an acknowledgement that they are not ready to change but that you will revisit this another day. They might not be ready today but might be ready at a later date.

Contemplation – parents are interested in change and are actively considering making a change but are indecisive (ambivalent) about changing.

Next step: Parents need to decide about changing and may need to find good reasons, shared values, and desires to support changing their behaviour.

Tips:

- Don't get stuck on the reasons they don't want to change (ambivalence)

- Focus on, and stress the benefits of changing

- Elicit from them what might shift them towards 6 or 7 on the Ruler

		• What might some important reasons be for moving towards 7?
		Preparation – parents, are moving away from contemplating and are close to making a commitment or decision about what to do. **Next Step:** To move forward and build their commitment to change, parents will need to begin to plan for the change they are going to make. **Tips:** • Don't just hand the parents a ready-made plan which they did not help to prepare. • Don't seek to engage them in a plan which they might find too challenging. • Focus on their commitment, activity, and the steps they will be taking. • Discuss their plan for change, work in partnership to make the plan, setting specific time frames for making changes. Practitioners need to focus on the child so making changes might need to be quick to prevent further harm.
		Action – preparing for action sees the parents getting ready to make changes or have already begun to do so. **Next Step:** They will need support to continue to build on their commitment with a realistic action plan. **Tips:** • Work with parents to resolve problems that are causing barriers to effect change. • Work with parents to make sure the plan is specific and that everyone involves understands what outcomes they aim to achieve with timescales for making the change. Parents must have a clear idea of how they plan to make the change.

		• Support them to manage any indecision or ambivalence that might arise.
 		Maintenance – Parents are continuing to take action, and their changed or new behaviours have replaced the old ones. **Next Step:** This is about maintaining the change, and parents may need continued support until things are stable and the chance of relapse has significantly decreased. **Tips:** • Work with parents to resolve difficulties and deal with relapse. • What might hinder continued success and work on minimising or getting rid of them • Identify support from family and friends who are willing to support the parents to keep the momentum going or maintain the changes. Note: consider a Family Group Conference (FGC).

Readiness to Change Ruler

Assessing where the parents' readiness or willingness to change. Below each heading, write the parents' comments or observations to help continue the conversation and move them along the ruler.

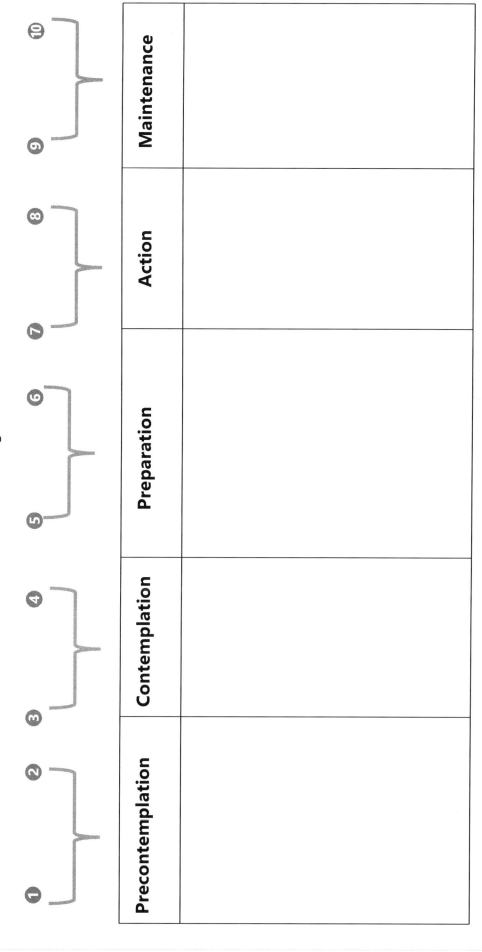

Precontemplation	Contemplation	Preparation	Action	Maintenance

6.5 How Do You Respond to Conflict – Questionnaire[27]

When parents find themselves in situations where they disagree or have a different view, they are likely to respond a certain way:

a) Accommodate	=	I lose, you win
b) Avoid	=	You lose, I lose
c) Collaborate	=	I win, you win
d) Compromise	=	both win some, both lose some
e) Control/Compete	=	I win, you lose

Using the statements below, think about how you would respond to the situation being described. Check the ratings that correspond to the answer. Discuss the responses and their implications.

When we disagree:	Always	Sometimes	Never
1. I am usually firm in following my goals	☐	☐	☐
2. I try to win my point of view	☐	☐	☐
3. I give up some points in exchange for others	☐	☐	☐
4. I feel that differences are not always worth worrying out	☐	☐	☐
5. I try to find a position that is between others' and mine	☐	☐	☐
6. I try to consider the other person's wishes in negotiations	☐	☐	☐

---

27 Adapted from K. W. Thomas, "Toward Multidimensional Values in Teaching: The Example of Conflict Behaviours," *Academy of Management Review 2* (1977), Table 1, p. 487 - 9.

7. I try to show the logic and benefits of my position	☐	☐	☐
8. I always lean toward a direct discussion of the problem	☐	☐	☐
9. I try to find a fair combination of gains and losses for both of us	☐	☐	☐
10. I attempt to work through our differences immediately	☐	☐	☐
11. I try to avoid creating unpleasantness for myself	☐	☐	☐
12. I might try to soothe others' feelings and preserve our relationship	☐	☐	☐
13. I attempt to get all concerns and issues dealt with immediately	☐	☐	☐
14. I sometimes avoid taking positions that create controversy	☐	☐	☐
15. I try not to hurt others' feelings	☐	☐	☐
Scoring: Always = 1 **Sometimes = 2** **Never = 3**			

6.6 How Do You Respond to Conflict – Cards

The preceding statements can be turned into a card game and used to capture the views. It might be preferable for some people as a questionnaire is usually off-putting for some parents. There are some blank cards to add additional statements.

I am usually firm in pursuing my goals	I try to win my position
I give up some points in exchange for others	I feel that differences are not always worth worrying out
I try to find a position that is between others' and mine	In approaching a negotiation, I try to consider the other person's wishes

I try to show the logic and benefits of my position

I always lean toward a direct discussion of the problem

I try to find a fair combination of gains and losses for both of us

I attempt to work through our differences immediately

I try to avoid creating unpleasantness for myself

I might try to soothe others' feelings and preserve our relationship

I attempt to get all concerns and issues dealt with immediately

I sometimes avoid taking positions that create controversy

I try not to hurt the others' feelings

Just remember the following key behaviours to use when managing conflict:

- Deal with issues, not personalities

- Take responsibility for yourself and your participation

- Communicate openly

- Avoid placing blame

- Listen actively

- Sort out the issues

- Stay focused on the present; don't dwell on the past

- Weigh up the consequences

- Identify resolution options

- Develop an outcome and obtain consensus.

- Suppose that you follow all of these suggestions and you still are confronted with that problematic situation or that difficult person.

6.7 Relationship Scaling Tool

The relationship scaling tool is for parents to individually rank their **present** level of satisfaction with their relationship. The tool is designed to help parents think about what they want to change.

As you can see the assessment tool is partially populated; however, there is a blank tool that you can ask parents to complete. This will allow them to tell you what they are unhappy about.

Populated Version

On a scale of **1** to **10** circle, the number you feel reflects your present level of **satisfaction** with each part of your life. Then write down what you feel needs to change

Sex/Intimacy

①	②	③	④	⑤	⑥	⑦	⑧	⑨	⑩

What needs to change?

Communication: *The way we talk to each other*

①	②	③	④	⑤	⑥	⑦	⑧	⑨	⑩

What needs to change?

Parenting: *Our parenting style*

①	②	③	④	⑤	⑥	⑦	⑧	⑨	⑩

What needs to change?

Household chores: *sharing responsibility for doing chores*

①	②	③	④	⑤	⑥	⑦	⑧	⑨	⑩

What needs to change?

Social Media: *Inappropriate use or amount of time spent on Social Media*

①	②	③	④	⑤	⑥	⑦	⑧	⑨	⑩

What needs to change?

Blank Relationship Scaling Tool

In the line above the numbers, insert what you believe is causing conflict between you. Then on a scale of **1** to 10 circle the number that you feel reflects your present level of **satisfaction** with that part of your life. Think about what you feel needs to change and add it in the section provided

①	②	③	④	⑤	⑥	⑦	⑧	⑨	⑩

What needs to change?

①	②	③	④	⑤	⑥	⑦	⑧	⑨	⑩

What needs to change?

①	②	③	④	⑤	⑥	⑦	⑧	⑨	⑩

What needs to change?

①	②	③	④	⑤	⑥	⑦	⑧	⑨	⑩

What needs to change?

①	②	③	④	⑤	⑥	⑦	⑧	⑨	⑩

What needs to change?

①	②	③	④	⑤	⑥	⑦	⑧	⑨	⑩

What needs to change?

6.8 A Road Map to Damaging Your Relationship

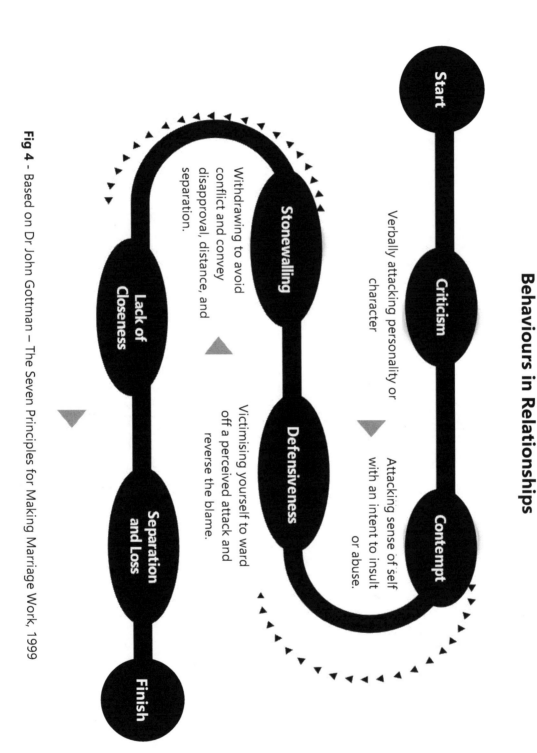

Behaviours in Relationships

Start

Criticism

Verbally attacking personality or character

Contempt

Attacking sense of self with an intent to insult or abuse.

Defensiveness

Victimising yourself to ward off a perceived attack and reverse the blame.

Stonewalling

Withdrawing to avoid conflict and convey disapproval, distance, and separation.

Lack of Closeness

Separation and Loss

Finish

Fig 4 - Based on Dr John Gottman – The Seven Principles for Making Marriage Work, 1999

I mentioned John Gottman's analogy of the 'four horsemen of the apocalypse.' According to Gottman, 'criticism, contempt, defensiveness and stonewalling' **(fig 4)** are gauges of relationship failure with 93% accuracy in predicting divorce (parental separation).

Gottman suggested that there are antidotes to the behaviours mentioned above. These suggestions are in the section (Part III) with tools to support parents.

Assuming poor communication is at the heart of these behaviours, parents will need to adjust their behaviours and the way they communicate. When assessing to identify the problem, understanding how the parents speak to or behave towards each other is critical as it will inform the intervention.

6.9 Stages of Relationship

Understanding where the parents are in their relationship is critical to identifying what is happening and contributing to the parental conflict.

Different versions of relationship stages exist that reflects the creator's ideas and may or may not be appropriate for all parents. The reason being nowadays, relationships are very diverse and take different routes. It will be necessary for you to assess the stage the couples are at in the relationship. You cannot assume that a couple's relationship follows specific steps. Some of the relationship models are based on marriage stages and might not be appropriate to the parents you support.

Some stages of a relationship are in **fig 6** below:

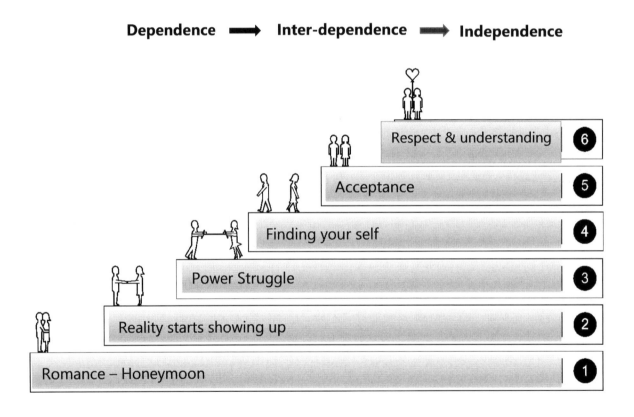

Fig 6 – Relationship Stages

There are different ways of looking at the stages of a relationship. It is crucial to consider other views because relationships can be very diverse and do not follow a distinct pathway.

For professionals, the most challenging job is to get parents on the same page of willingness to work together on their relationship at the same time.

This section of the toolkit provides an overview of what might be happening at different stages of the parents' relationship. It is not a tool for intervention or guidance on couple counselling but a simple overview to help Practitioners discuss relationship dynamics they may be observing.

Some relationships start healthy and become unhealthy and then go into decline. They then follow predictable deterioration stages and patterns. What happens to the relationship will depend on the couple's actions and intentions. One person is unhappy with the relationship but is not sure they want to end it, and the other person is fighting to save the relationship.

Such uncertainty and different views can cause tensions and conflict in the relationship. Parents' relationship quality has such a profound impact on children that Practitioners need to understand what is happening through discussions with the parents to provide appropriate intervention.

Providing information about these stages of the relationship could help couples understand where their relationship is now and where it might be heading. Having an insight might motivate them to access support.

Stage One – The Healthy Relationship

Practitioners will know from experience that many relationships don't start in the same way. However, for this section, I am talking about relationships that started where both parents wanted to be together, believe they were in love and decide to have children together. Both were planning to spend the rest of their lives together and hope to have a great future.

Stage Two – Disillusionment/Reality

Also, call the reality stage because one person in the relationship realises, they are unhappy or that there is something wrong in the relationship. The disillusioned partner might not tell anyone because they think that all relationships go through a sticky patch, and it might pass - not serious.

As they continue to feel disillusioned, the relationship slips further into deterioration. The partner begins to consider separation because they continue to be unhappy, and the problem is getting more serious. At this stage, they may disregard the idea of separation for multiple reasons, including having children together.

Other factors like values, beliefs, religion, and financial status, and many more might influence their decision.

The uncertainty can lead to one partner backing away from the other. Snide remarks, contempt, and criticism might appear in the relationship, and conflict escalates.

Stage Three – Detachment

The unhappy person tells the other that separation is not an option and starts to find ways to cope with the situation. They begin to search for distractions and interests they can pursue to keep themselves busy. Social media, joining dating websites, hobbies, gym, working late, and even having an affair are things they might use as distractions.

They are unhappy but think they can deal with their situation if they can direct their attention elsewhere.

The conflict continues in the home, becoming more intensive and frequent, and they are not cooperating with each other.

At this stage, the couple might involve friends and family in their situation, and the conflict continues to escalate even further (see the conflict escalator diagram).

Often it is not enough to counteract their unhappiness, so the unhappy partner pulls away entirely. They might reveal their sadness and uncertainty about remaining in the relationship.

The "happy" partner might sense something is wrong with the relationship but might not understand that it is due to their partner's unhappiness.

When the unhappy partner turns away from the relationship, this is where the relationship crisis begins.

Stage Four – The Rejected Partner Panics

The unhappy partner reveals the truth about why they have been pulling away. They are not happy and unsure about remaining in the relationship. "Attachment Panic" sets in because the person you are attached to is pulling away from you and is at high risk of leaving for good. Some people cope with this by giving the unhappy partner breathing space they may have asked for while spending energy working on themselves.

Beware, at this stage, conflict can intensify, and the children get exposed to destructive parental conflict. Parents will need professional intervention for themselves and to protect the children from the impact of parental conflict.

Stage Five – The Decider Flees

The rejected spouse continues to pursue their unhappy partner, but this makes matters worse. They are determined, more than ever, to leave the relationship. Often, the aggrieved spouse decides to end the relationship at this point or at least separate.

It will take some time for the rejected spouse to give up hope that they can win their partner back. They may need counselling to come to terms with what has happened.

Children caught up in this situation may also need help to come to terms with their experiences. Given the 'deciders' decision, there is a strong possibility that parental conflict will continue. Their children will get caught up and used in the parents' conflict about, for example, contact or access and maintenance.

Stage Six – The Rejected Partner Gives Up

The rejected partner gives up hope of reconciliation and shows signs of recovering and getting on with their life.

Though both partners might be getting on with their lives, there is a real danger that things are not going well for the children. There is an ongoing situation where they are caught up in the middle and used as messengers and spies.

Professionals working with children need to be alert to the dangers for children.

Conflict can continue where both or one of the partners has a new partner or family. Co-parenting interventions and support are critical to ensure children's stability and security.

Stage Seven - The Decider Returns

Some people do reconcile after leaving their relationship. If this is happening, Practitioners should encourage the partners to access support to avoid making the same mistakes.

Impact on Children

Parents need to be aware of how the responses and reactions to what is going on in their relationship can negatively impact their children as the conflict becomes destructive.

Children may be exposed to destructive conflict, and parents' behaviour can impact the quality of care. The argument develops as an unhappy partner is less supportive in the home.

Be aware! At this stage, experienced workers might detect the onset of parental alienation. It is crucial to identify and intervene as the implication can be detrimental to children.

Is the Relationship in Difficulties or Distressed?

Before moving forward, it is timely to reiterate the point about outcomes for children. We know that a growing body of research evidences the importance of parental relationships' quality on children's development and positive outcomes. Where this is managed and resolved well, it is known to affect children's development positively. However, if the conflict between parents is "frequent, intense and unresolved." However, if the conflict between parents is frequent, intense, and unresolved,"[28] this can negatively affect children's long-term outcomes.

---

[28] (Gordon, Acquah, Sellers, & Chowdry, 2016)

6.10 Relationship Scaling

Mark on the scale where you feel or believe your relationship is as a couple. One (1) is very distressed, and 5 and below means there are some problems in the relationship, while 6 to 10 means things are going in the right direction; however, at 6 to 7, you may still feel you need some relationship support.

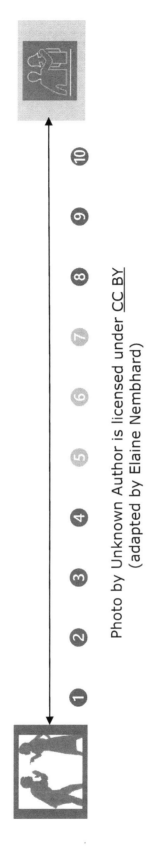

Photo by Unknown Author is licensed under <u>CC BY</u>
(adapted by Elaine Nembhard)

It can also help parents think about where they are now and what they would like to be using **motivational** and **solution-focused questions to help look to an ideal future.**

1. How was life before the problem?

2. What is happening in the relationship now?

3. What needs to change? What would you and your partner do differently?

4. What could prevent you from making changes?

5. What would the relationship be like if things were to change?

6. What would be happening? How would you know things are going well?

7. How would you maintain the changes you have made?

6.11 Relationship See-Saw

The 'relationship (see-saw) can help with the relationship scaling exercise. It is also useful to assess if there are power imbalances in the relationship, in which case the see-saw would be seriously unbalanced. Comparing relationships to sitting on a **'see-saw'** is a good way to view relationships – they have their ups and downs. The relationship can tip to one side, and parents need to get it to balance. What each person does on the 'see-saw' will affect the other person. The non-distressed or healthy relationship is balanced and is where both parents share the responsibilities for and in the relationship.

By unknown Author is licensed under CC BY
(adapted by Elaine Nembhard)

Getting the Balance Right

- Equality in responsibilities features in the relationship
- Each person knows to take things in turn
- Things feel right and are working well
- There are stability and predictable routines
- Each person is not trying to control the relationship
- Love and concern for the other person
- No pushing to change the other person
- Give and take

We all have our ups and downs. In a healthy relationship, we don't really try to stop ourselves from having the ups and downs –we go with the flow. There is always a movement - up or down; how couples manage those ups and down will determine what happens in the relationship.

Tips on using the see-saw:

- Practitioners can use the '**see-saw**' to start a conversation about what is causing an imbalance in the relationship.

- If you have ever been on a '**see-saw**,' you know that if you jump off, the other person will most likely fall **off** to the ground.   You don't want anyone to fall off, so the balance has to be restored.

- The '**see – saw**' can become unbalanced because things are not shared; one person may be doing more housework than the other, have more leisure time, provide most of the care for the children.

6.12 Relationship Wheel

You may already be familiar with the **Duluth Model** on domestic abuse, of which there are numerous examples and adaptions on the internet. Here we have adapted the idea to show factors that make up **a 'healthy relationship'** to guide Practitioners to work with parents.

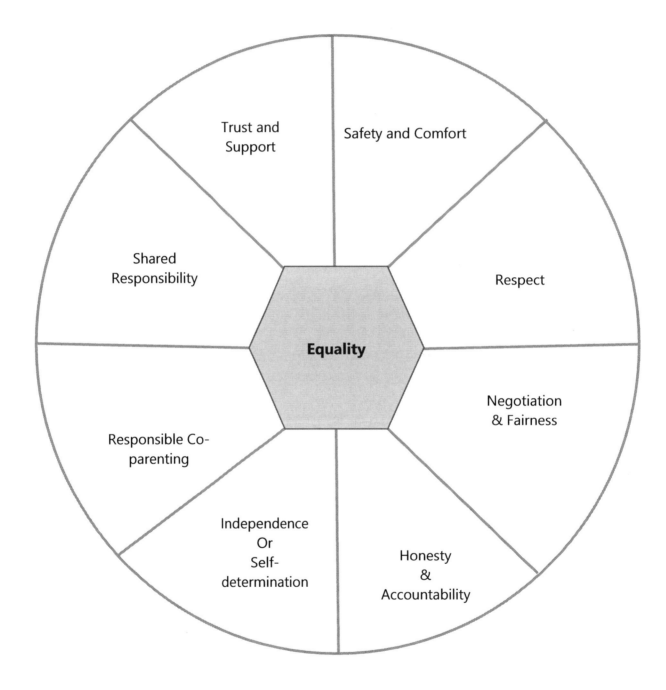

Adapted from the Domestic Abuse Intervention Project, Duluth, MN, www.deluth-model.org

Explanation

Trust & Support

- Supports your passions
- Is emotionally affirming and understanding
- Respects your right to your feelings, friends, activities, and opinions
- Supports your goals

Safety & Comfort

- Ensures you can express yourself
- Intentionally creates an environment where you feel safe
- Ensures you can do the things you want to do

Respect

- Is emotionally affirming and understanding
- Listens non-judgmentally
- Values your opinions

Negotiation & Fairness

- Accepts change
- Seeks mutually satisfying resolutions to conflict
- Is willing to compromise
- Can agree to disagree

Honesty & Accountability

- Both of you accept responsibility for yourselves
- Both of you admit when you are wrong
- Both of you communicate openly and truthfully

Independence

- Gives each other room to breathe
- Both of you take time alone when you need it
- Neither of you expects the other to give you everything you need.
- Neither of you expects the other to solve all the problems.

Responsible Parenting

Responsible parenting is about effective co-parenting relationships whether parents are together or separated. It includes:

- Agree and implement boundaries and routines
- Count on each other to maintain commitments
- Show willingness to be flexible
- Collaborate as parents
- Agree on the most important things concerning the children
- Avoid engaging in manipulating behaviours and parental alienation activities
- Communicate about any last-minute changes in a healthy way
- Do not use children against one another
- Recognise and appreciate each other's purpose

Shared Responsibility

- Undertake fair share of the responsibilities in the relationship
- Undertake fair share of chores in the home
- Take responsibility to sort out tension and conflict situations.

6.13 What Are Some Signs of a Relationship In Distress

Thinking about the 'healthy relationship wheel,' you can use the following diagram to work with the parents to examine aspects of the couple's relationship that are not going well and causing conflict. You may need to consider other issues depending on what is happening or what they tell you.

Couples can complete this independently and then compare their ratings. They can potentially find areas that they agree on, and areas they consider need support or additional work.

Relationship Wheel

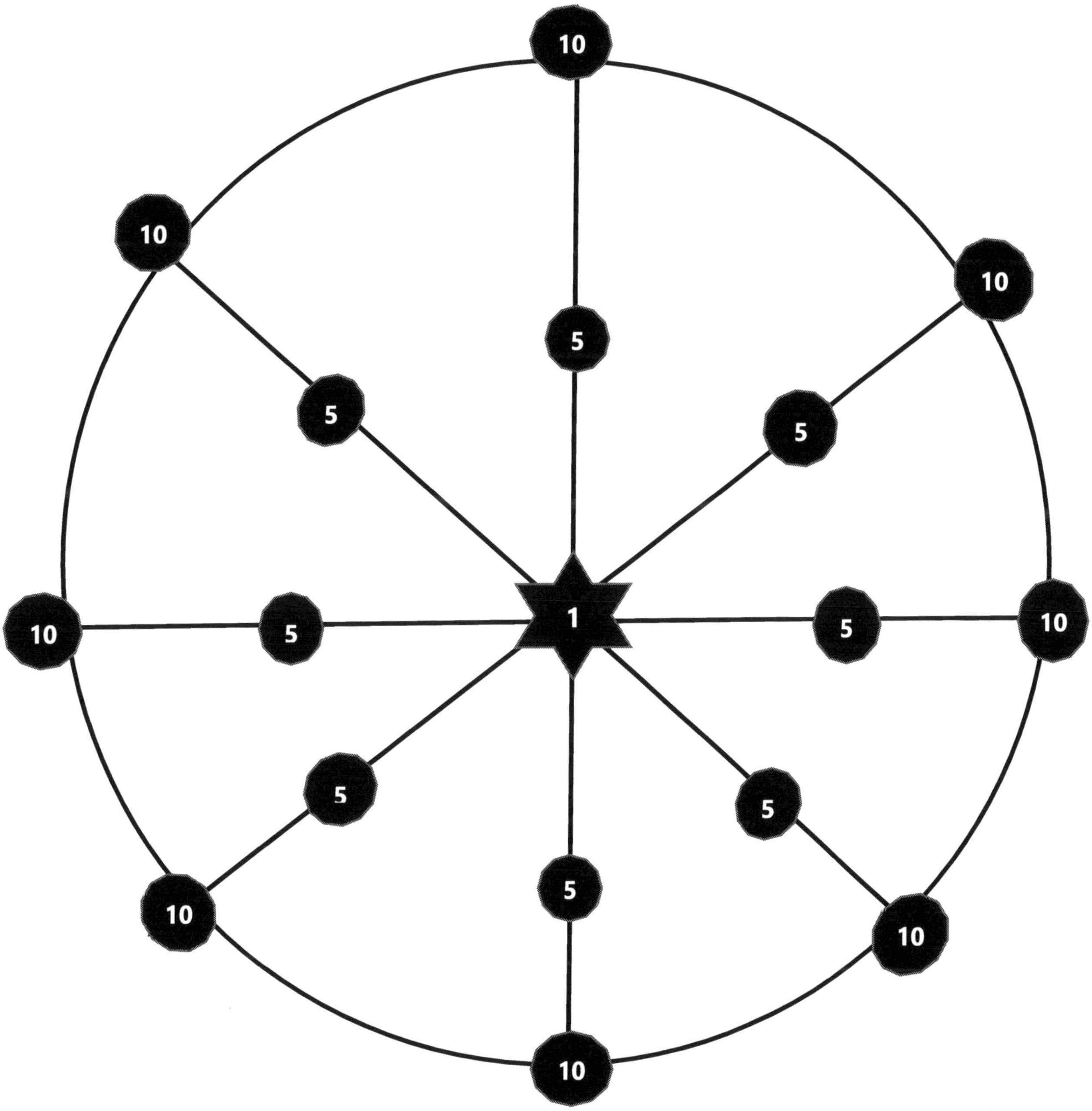

The use of the relationship scale may lead to various issues that need response:

- How did they do?

- Are the scores different?

- Use the results to start exploring what needs to change and what support the couple might need?

7. Solutions - Teaching Skills to Manage Destructive conflict

We have now identified the problem, causes of the problem and are now preparing to do something about it.

One way of helping parents is to enhance their ability to manage conflict situations constructively by teaching them conflict resolution skills. Practitioners in early support services or similar settings are in an excellent position to help parents understand the impact of conflict on children and develop their conflict resolution skills.

Involving Fathers

From my experience working on the front line of child protection and training Practitioners working with families, I know that involving fathers in their work is difficult. There has been a tendency to work primarily with mothers even though fathers have an active role in their children's lives. Professionals always have an explanation for this phenomenon; however, one reason is a lack of effort to involve the father. As we now know from research, the fathers' role is significant to the children's development and needs to be valued. Change can only happen if professionals consistently treat fathers and mothers as equals, given the growing body of research evidence that fathers' involvement in their children's lives positively influences their development in many ways.

Some key points

"Father-child relationships, be they positive, negative or lacking, have profound and wide-ranging impacts on children that last a lifetime." *(Department of Work and Pensions, 2007)*

"Fathers play a crucial role in child development and subsequent adult status and behaviour" *(Flouri, 2005)*

"Fathers are far more than just "second adults" in the home. Involved fathers ... bring positive benefits that no other person is as likely to bring" *(Popenoe, 1996)*

The Fatherhood Institute has a wealth of evidence showing the value of fathers. If you are interested, have a look at their website: www.fatherhoodinstitute.org/research

- NOTES -

Part III - Tools for Working with Parents to Make Changes

The tools in this section are varied and the Practitioner will need to select the tool that they and the parents feel will work best.   Some of the tools can be given to parents to carry out self-assessments.

List of Tools

Conflict Tree

Common Grounds – The PIN Model

Counteract the 4 Horsemen of the Apocalypse

Thoughts, Feelings, and Behavioural Responses

What we Argue About and the Intensity of the Arguments

Quality of the Parental Relationship

Couple's Relationship SWOT Analysis

Knowing When Conflict Occurs and its Cause

How We See Our Relationship - Parents' Perspective

8.1 The Conflict Tree

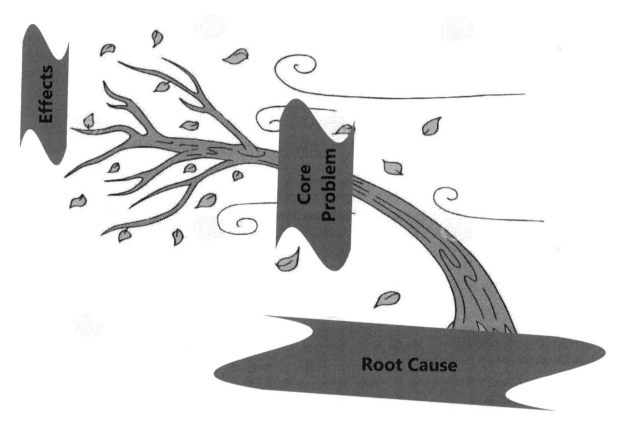

Modified by Elaine Photo which is by an unknown Author is licensed under CC BY-SA-NC

How to use it

The Practitioner can use the tree either with individuals, couples in a workshop setting. The tool works well with parents who are visually and artistically inclined. It is a simple, fun tool to help understand the causes and effects of parental conflict and get at the core of the problem.

Separate the issues, organise them into categories, figure out the priorities, and make a plan of action to make the desired changes. This approach is effective in dealing with complex conflict.

Workshops

In workshops, you can use flipcharts, pens, and post-it notes. Ask participants to draw a large tree on the paper, including roots. Write on different colour post-it notes the root causes, the core problem, and the effects and post them appropriately.

Once completed, identify the 'effects' that need to be dealt with immediately and which causes need to be addressed to alter the core problem.

8.2 Common Grounds – The PIN Model

(Positions, Interests, and Needs)

When there is parental conflict, we would ideally want parents to achieve a **"Win-Win"** situation. Achieving this involves listening and understanding the other person's position and needs and leading to creative and meaningful ways of resolving conflict.

It helps parents move away from an irreconcilable position and focus on shared interests and needs.

What is the problem?

My side (name) ....

My side (name) ....

My Interests

My Interest

Shared Interests:

Shared Needs:

How to use it

Things mapped in the diagram must be linked to the issue causing the conflict – the problem.

All that is needed is for the parents to map all the positions, interests, and needs. Then work together to find where there are shared interests and needs.

The Practitioner can help the parents to move away from their positions and focus on what they have in common; their shared interests and needs.

Conclude the exercise by finding ways to get the parents in the conflict to move away from their respective position and find alternative solutions that focus on what they have in common, e.g., shared interests and needs.

Note, if parents are unable to find something they agreed on, the Practitioner can highlight that they have a child or children together and have their best interest at heart. Reflecting on what is best for their children may enough to move them away from the issue that is causing the conflict.

8.3 Counteract the 4 Horsemen of the Apocalypse

According to Dr. Gottman, the roadmap to damaging relationships is [29]Criticism, Contempt, Defensiveness, and Stonewalling. Dr. Gottman provided suggestions on the antidote to these behaviours. You will see suggestions about using **"I Statements"** – these are also included as a tool to work with parents to assist positive communication.

Negative Behaviours	Suggested Solutions
Criticism Attack the **character** of the person or question their **intention**.	Deal with the **specific behaviours** without blame or attacking the person. Use "**I Statements**" to communicate.
Contempt Treating the other person with **disrespect** or **ridicule**.	Communicate what you **value** in the other person, even if you disagree. Attempt to **understand** the person's **perspective**.
Defensiveness Shifting the focus from the problem onto the other person's flaws.	Take ownership of your contribution to the problem. Focus on **your impact**, **NOT** on your intentions (self-defence) or the other's action/attack.
Stonewall **Withdrawing** from the interaction, **shutting down**, or **checking out**	Softly **tell** the other that you are feeling "**overwhelmed**" and need a **break** (define time limits). Do whatever helps you **calm yourself**, then **come back to resume**.

---

[29] (Gottman & Silver, 2015)

The following tool is used in cognitive behavioural therapy to stop the vicious cycle of negative thinking and feeling. It can help parents identify their thoughts, feelings, and behaviour in interaction with their partner.

This model can help couples recognise how they internalise behaviour that they observe, which in turn affects how they feel, impacting their response.

It is helpful to help couples understand each other's behaviour. The idea is that:

Thoughts create feelings $\longrightarrow$ Feelings create behaviour $\longrightarrow$ Behaviour reinforces thoughts

Situation/Trigger

- Stressors in the parental relationship.
- (What vital relationship needs are not being met?)

Thoughts and Perception

- What do you think that behaviour means?
- How could we test whether what I think is true?

Feelings

- What emotions are you feeling?

Behaviour

- How do you behave, what do you do?

Beck's model seeks to view the relationship between the behaviour that we observe, our thoughts, the feelings generated, and the behavioural response. For example:

Observed behaviour: When you spend a lot of time on social media.

Thoughts: I think this means that you are talking with someone you find more interesting than me.

Feelings: This makes me feel unloved, unimportant, and rejected.

Behavioural or response: I get annoyed and irritable, which invariably develops into an argument between us.

8.4 Thoughts, Feelings and Behavioural Response Template

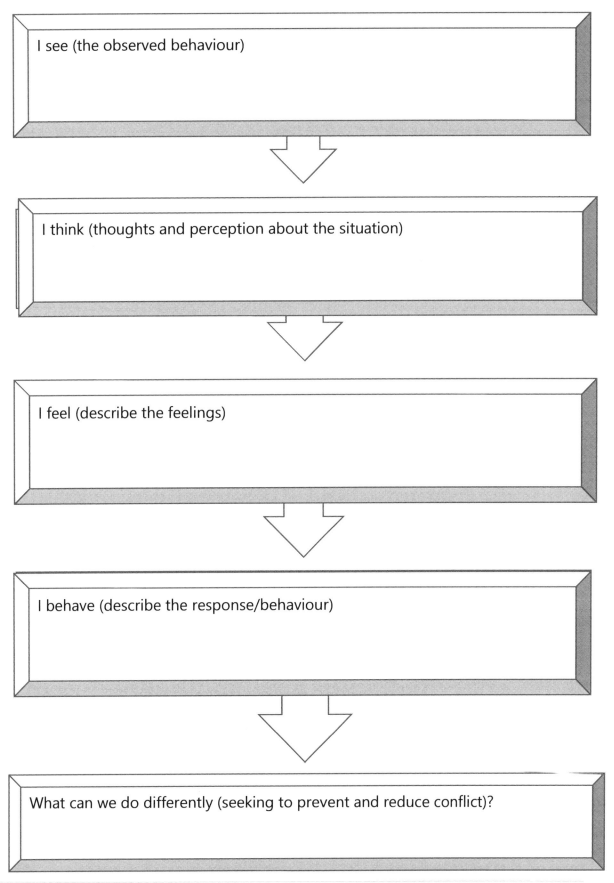

I see (the observed behaviour)

I think (thoughts and perception about the situation)

I feel (describe the feelings)

I behave (describe the response/behaviour)

What can we do differently (seeking to prevent and reduce conflict)?

Using the template to express their feelings can help parents understand how arguments start and can escalate - explaining how the relationship between thoughts, feelings, and behavioural response can help them understand why someone may behave in a certain way. It should encourage them to start thinking about what changes they could make to prevent or reduce conflict between them.

Its application can also help parents acknowledge their thoughts and challenge their assumptions and perceptions about the observed behaviour. There may be a good reason why the person is on social media or may not understand how it makes the other person feel. Opening up the conversation increases the chance of finding a way to deal satisfactorily with the situation.

8.5 What We Argue About and the Intensity of the Arguments

Using the scale, ascertain either by direct work with the parties to the conflict or self-assessment what they usually argue about, the frequency and intensity or the arguments.

Remember the conflict escalator? Things are beginning to get difficult and need attention before it continues up the escalator.

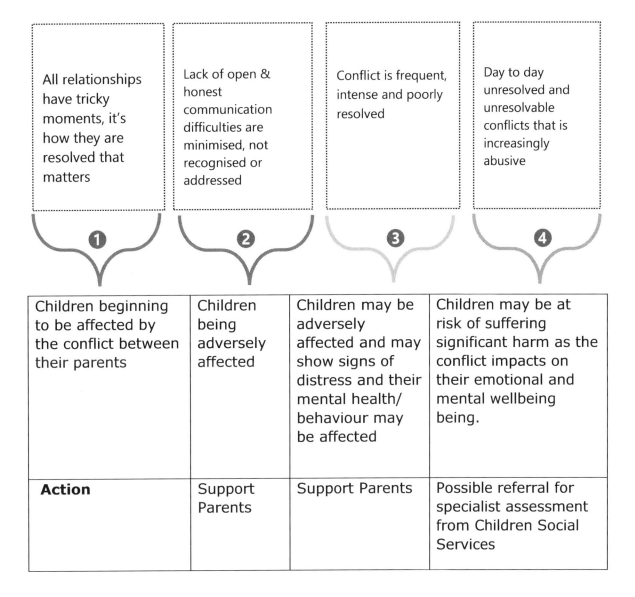

All relationships have tricky moments, it's how they are resolved that matters	Lack of open & honest communication difficulties are minimised, not recognised or addressed	Conflict is frequent, intense and poorly resolved	Day to day unresolved and unresolvable conflicts that is increasingly abusive
❶	❷	❸	❹
Children beginning to be affected by the conflict between their parents	Children being adversely affected	Children may be adversely affected and may show signs of distress and their mental health/ behaviour may be affected	Children may be at risk of suffering significant harm as the conflict impacts on their emotional and mental wellbeing being.
Action	Support Parents	Support Parents	Possible referral for specialist assessment from Children Social Services

Intensity and impact on children

Once you have the issues that are causing conflict, you will need to support the parties to resolve their conflict. You might not be in a position to resolve the conflict but could make a referral to specialist services.

8.6 Quality of the parental relationship

Having ascertained the things that, the couple tend to argue about, you will need to learn more about **them,** their family, and the arguments' context. You might want to consider exploring the **relationship's strengths** or, more importantly, the parental relationship quality. It might seem repetitive, but it must be the intervention's primary focus, hence the reminder throughout the toolkit.

The inter-parental relationship's quality, specifically how parents communicate and relate to each other, is increasingly recognised as a primary influence on effective parenting practices and children's long-term mental health and future life chances.

Practitioners operate in a problem-oriented world, focusing almost entirely on finding problems and finding solutions or interventions. Similarly, the couples you are working with are likely to have a clear picture of what is wrong with their relationship but haven't spent any time considering their strengths as a couple.

For this exercise, everyone involved **MUST** forget the **problem-orientated** approach and focus primarily on the **strengths**. By focusing on the strengths, it is envisaged that these can be strengthened even more and result in a stronger bond between them.

We have used this approach with working with couples and their children with children (8 years and upwards), giving their views about the couple's relationship. People are usually surprised to learn about their strengths because they are generally preoccupied with the wrong things.

8.7 Couple's Relationship SWOT Analysis

You can do this separately or together. Your approach will depend on a number of variables such as couple availability and willingness to engage. Using the template below, work through a personal SWOT analysis with the couple. You may already be familiar with the concept of completing a SWOT, but just in case you are not familiar with what SWOT (self-explanatory) stands for:

Strengths	The first thing to do with the couple is to get them to list their strengths. This will hopefully build their confidence and focus on the good things in their relationship.
Weaknesses	These will be the things that the couple don't do so well, e.g., such as being open about how they feel and spending quality time together. Also, the weakness could be an inability to see and acknowledge the strengths.
Opportunities	Opportunities come in different shapes and forms. When it knocks, you should grab it with both hands, but sometimes opportunities pass by you without you even noticing them. So, you need to look out for those opportunities that can support the couple's relationship.
Threats	Look at threats as disguised opportunities, so you need to use them to change what you don't like. Threats can negatively affect your relationship, so it's vital to anticipate the threats and take action against them before your relationship becomes a casualty or victim.

Once you complete the SWOT, you can follow up with the couple's activity plan or improvement plan.

Couple's Relationship SWOT Analysis

a) Completing the **SWOT** should the couple to issues that might threaten their relationship, either from themselves or outside the relationship.

b) Encourage the couple to choose any areas, including **strengths** that they think could be better.

Crucially it is essential to get their commitment, and therefore, it is necessary to ask:

- What are they going to work on to improve the quality of their relationship?

- How are they going to achieve this?

- What are they going to do to achieve what they want to achieve?

Couples can develop an activity plan to cover any areas of their SWOT. The idea is to identify **strengths** and find areas for potential growth. As the Practitioner, you may play a role in supporting the couple to achieve their goals.

Monitoring progress

Someone needs to take on the role of monitoring progress, and therefore you may need to agree to this – remember what gets measured gets done. Encourage the couple to set a date to get together to talk about progress or journey in a relaxed and friendly manner. Say, about a month from completing the activity plan.

Working template on the following page

	Strengths	Weaknesses	
Internal			Internal
	Opportunities	Threats	
External			External

S	W	O	T
Strength	Weaknesses	Opportunities	Threats

8.8 Knowing When Conflict Occurs and its Cause

Knowing when conflict is likely to occur will also help identify the trigger and cause. What is happening and when:

- In the morning?
- In the afternoon?
- In the evening?
- Is it in the night?
- Also, it can identify the day of the week insight into a pattern of behaviour.

The template helps parents explore what is happening as they go about their daily lives. It can be used to monitor just one day or an entire week and what has triggered the conflict. It is a way to help parents pay attention to what is happening, their behaviours and responses, and take steps to change things.

When/Time	Day	Details of what happened

How We See Our Relationship - Parents' Perspective

Below are some statements regarding relationships. These cards can be copied, cut-out, and given to parents if they feel they want to work on their relationship. They can be used to ask the couple to identify which of the cards

    (1)   applies to them
    (2)   which ones does not and,
    (3)   which ones they would like to work on or have in their lives going forward.

Caring for each other My partner pays attention to my feelings and needs and always offer support.	**Respect for each other** My partner accepts me for who I am even when we when have disagreements.
Respect for individuality My partner respects me as an individual and as an equal and treats me with care and respect.	**Physical & emotional Care** My partner takes care to make sure my physical and emotional needs are met and not ignored.
Tolerance or Acceptance My partner understands that we can have different views and I don't I have to agree with them.	**Playfulness** I can freely use playful gesture (clowning, romping around) and overtures without *misunderstanding*

Humour
My partner used humour in our relationship but it is never aggressive (making fun of the person so its hurtful).

Put-downs and sarcasm
My partner rarely uses put-downs/sarcasm but never to control me or use deliberate hostility disguised as humour.

Self-Esteem
My partner does not do anything to damage my self-esteem.

A feeling of security
My partner offers support and I know I can lean on them when I am feeling vulnerable, low and, or stressed.

Safety
I am comfortable sharing my thoughts, feelings, and ideas with my partner, without fear of being put down, shut down, ridiculed, or criticised, or told to act, or feel differently.

Physically& Emotionally Connected
I feel emotionally and physically connected in many ways to my partner and the feelings are shared.

Trust
I trust my partner to be loyal and can rely and confide in them because I feel safe knowing they won't betray me.

Honesty
I trust my partner and can be totally open with them and don't feel I have to hide who I am or what I think and feel.

Dependability
My partner is dependable in many ways like helping with the children, paying bills, and caring for the home.

Fidelity or Faithfulness
My partner and I trust each other to be faithful to each other and so far, things have worked well.

We are family
We work together amicably to share family responsibilities and to care for our children.

Sacrifice
Sacrifice raises questions of power imbalance. Do you find yourself always making sacrifices and your partner isn't willing to do the same?

Sharing Responsibilities
My partner shares all the responsibilities for raising our children and also our goals for them.

Compromise
When there is a situation that is causing problems, my partner and I are able to compromise in order to resolve it.

Discussion rather than lectures
My partner and I discuss things together rather one person talking at the other because they feel they know best.

Negative communication
When we try to communicate there are behaviours that increase conflict - contempt, *criticism, defensiveness, and emotional disconnect.*

Cooperation not Competition

We support each other and work as a team instead of competing against each other.

Non-blaming

We take responsibility for our actions instead of making excused or blame them on someone or something else.

Winner takes it all

When there is a disagreement, we can generally reach an agreement rather than there has to be a winner and a loser.

Compromise

When we compromise, it is fair and we both feel satisfied with the outcome as one person doesn't have to give up more than the other.

Agreeing to disagree

My partner and I sometimes disagree but can also agree to disagree instead of creating a drama out of nothing.

Difference

We accept that we are different people and do not have to be exactly the same.

Open communication

My partner and I can talk to each other openly feeling hurt and upset because we stay focused on the issue without making things personal.

Happiness

Happiness means different things to different people so we try to understand how each other is feeling and respect the way they are feeling.

Optimism

When things are not going well, we 'keep on going' and believe that things will get better in our relationship.

Expectation

When we started our relationship, we both hoped it would last and we will stay together and we are still hopeful that things will work out positively.

9. Positive Communication Strategies

This section cannot cover all communication styles, so we have limited it to focus on verbal communication as it is key to resolving conflict. In this section we will look at:

Characteristics of Passive, Aggressive and Assertive Communication

Using the P.A.U.S.E Approach in Personal Communication

Use of 'I' & 'YOU' Statements

Constructive Versus Destructive Communication

Characteristics of Passive, Aggressive and Assertive Communication

Passive		
Characteristics	**Outcome**	**Underlying Principle**
• Apologetic • An overly soft or tentative voice • Looking down or away • Stooped posture, excessive head nodding • Makes body smaller - stooped, leaning, hunched shoulders	• Careful to avoid conflict • Unwilling to express opinions, expectations, needs	*"My needs are less important than yours."*

Aggressive		
Characteristics	**Outcome**	**Underpinning Belief**
• Use 'You' statements • Loud voice, shouting • Staring or glaring • Makes body bigger upright, head high, shoulders out, hands-on hips, feet apart	• Seeks conflict • Expects others to agree with opinions and satisfy expectations, needs	*"Your needs are less important than mine."*

Assertive		
Characteristics	**Outcome**	**Underpinning Belief**
• Use 'I' statements • Firm voice • Looking directly (without staring) • Relaxed posture, smooth and relaxed movements • Open, welcoming stance	• Works to resolve conflict • Happy to express an opinion but also willing to listen to others • Willing to compromise and recognise that others may have different expectations and needs	"My needs are important, and your needs are important."

Using the P.A.U.S.E Approach in Personal Communication [30]

Many people will be aware of the power of pausing for a moment, no matter what we are doing. When we pause, take a break, we are giving ourselves the space to consider for a moment what to do next. In communicating in a conflict situation, a pause is critical to consider what comes next.

It creates the opportunity to consider the situation, make informed choices, and take control of your life. It leads us to listen more, talk less, and as a result, our relationships can improve with less conflict occurring.

For example, if one parent interrupts the other, they may immediately respond because they feel aggrieved, and they may say something in return that is hostile or unkind. However, if they were to pause for a moment and notice that they are feeling upset, they can then consider the other person's perspective and then choose the best response. It might be the same without a pause, but it might also be different. At least their response was considered and not an unconscious reaction.

The acronym P.A.U.S.E can help parents to discuss conflict situation in a meaningful way. It stands for:

P = Present   (The idea is about being **present** physically and mentally and remaining focus on the issue being discussed. So, it is better to have discussions when there are no distractions).

A= Acceptance   (Our perception of a situation can significantly influence our responses and choices in a conflict situation. It is vital to examine the facts as they are and **accept** them instead of reading into situations what we think is happening. One way of finding out the facts is to talk things through).

U= Undercurrent   (Parents can bring a lot of 'baggage', beliefs and values or **Undertones** (enduring vulnerabilities) to their relationship, and as the relationship evolve, some of these issues can be triggered and cause inter-parental conflict. Seek to be aware of any **undercurrent** or undertones so that these can be explored).

---

[30] (Puiman, 2019)

S= Synchronicity (If both parents want to create a win-win situation, they will need to have a similar mindset (**synchronicity or in sync**) and believe that a positive way forward will happen. In terms of inter-parental conflict, it will be vital for them always to be mindful of what is essential during their interaction. Hopefully, this will be their children and the parental relationship.

Ultimately, in a conflict situation, we would want parents to work together to build trust and remove any threats to the children's wellbeing and the integrity of their relationship).

S= Exchange (The final step in the P.A.U.S.E method is about **the exchange** with another person. Parents can use the *technique I feel, when you, because, I would like it if (introduced on pages 82-83)* to say what they want to say most honestly and sincerely. It is a powerful way for both parents to learn about and understand each other better, and thus reduce conflict.)

P.A.U.S.E just another way of saying STOP and is easier to remember – it stands for:

S - stop for a moment

T – take time to a deep or some deep breaths

O – observe and take not of how you are feeling and what you are thinking. Wait

before responding.

P – Proceed with more awareness and knowledge of the situation.

Use of 'I' & 'YOU' Statements

Like most people, when communicating their feelings about something or what we want from others, you may observe parents using 'YOU' statements. When a 'YOU' statement is used in communicating, it signifies fault and blame.

Here are some common examples of 'YOU' statements:

a) "You are late home again, causing the dinner to be ruined."
b) "Look at the damage you've done... I bet you did it on purpose."
c) You never want to spend quality time with me. anymore"
d) "The house is in the right state; no doubt you have been watching daytime TV instead of doing the cleaning?"

When someone uses these kinds of statements, it is highly likely to result in reactions such as **defensiveness** from the other person and provoke a counter-attack. It might not have been your intention, but chances are things will develop into an argument.

Doing things differently to change the communication pattern?

Think about what the person making the statement wants to accomplish. Do they want the other person to pay attention to them or to how they are feeling?

Though what they say could cause an argument, it might not have been what they intended.

Consider the earlier statements (a to d), what is the speaker trying to communicate.

Let's try and rephrase what was said to what might have been intended.

"YOU" Statement		Rephrase
"You are late again, causing the dinner to be ruined."		I went to a lot of trouble to make a nice dinner for the family, and I am really disappointed that we didn't get to eat together.
"You clumsy idiot, you've broken my favourite vase.		Can you please take care around my things? I really liked that vase, and I am upset that it got broken.
"You never want to spend quality time with me."		I feel that we are growing apart as we don't seem to spend any quality time together as we did before.

"The house is in a right state, what have you been doing all day?"	It would be good if you could spend some time cleaning the house while I am at work as it is rather messy and dirty.

Taking away the blaming and accusatory words and moderating the tone reflects what the person wants to communicate or accomplish. The new statements are less likely to produce a defensive or argumentative response and more likely to facilitate honest communication.

Making 'YOU' statements can be a way of avoiding having to acknowledge our feelings and placing the responsibility for how we feel onto someone else. 'I' statements make it clear how we feel. For this reason, it may seem as if they are exposing us or making us more vulnerable. Using 'I' statements' does take time until you get used to them, and they can become a valuable tool in communicating more assertively.

Risks in Using 'I' Statements

There is some risk in using 'I' as they involve asking the other person for what you. They are free to deny your request – say "no." Even though there is a risk, it is better to communicate what you want to say.

'I' statements are made up of four parts:

Expressing Your Self /Feelings ➡	**What**
I feel	*(taking responsibility for your feelings)*
When you[31]	*(stating the behaviour that is a problem)*
Because	*(what it is about the behaviour or its consequences that you don't like)*
I would really like it if	*(offering a preferred alternative or compromise)*

Use a similar formula (introduced on pages 82-83) to reframe 'YOU' statements. "**I feel** *sad and insecure (taking responsibility for your feelings)*

---

[31] US Dept of Health and Human Services (2005)

*"**when you** don't go out with me"* (stating the behaviour that is a problem)

*"**because** I want to spend time with you and be close"* (what it is about the behaviour or its consequences that you don't like)

*"**I would really like it if** we could do something together that we both enjoy"* (offering a preferred alternative or compromise)

This statement can be useful in opening up further conversation about the things you might enjoy doing together.

Common errors in constructing 'I' statements

Avoid inserting "that" or "like," *"I feel that ..."* or *"I feel like ..."* are words associated with **thought**, often an opinion or judgement. Both are usually followed by the word "you," as in "I feel that you don't care about me."

The use of "I feel" should always be followed by a **feeling** such as "sad," "glad," or "afraid."

1. **Avoid disguised 'YOU' statements**

   These include many sentences that begin with *"I feel that you ..."* or *"I feel like you ..."*

   If they haven't been preceded by some honest disclosure of the speaker's feelings, they will likely put the other person on the defensive.

2. **Avoid emphasising your negative feelings**

   Many people spend a significant amount of time communicating their negative feelings and forget to share positive emotions. Expressing your joy, happiness, relief, etc., when the other person has done something that elicits these feelings in you is equally important.

3. **Avoid understating the intensity of your feelings**

   When individuals first start working with 'I' statements, it is common for them to send a message that lessens their feelings' intensity. Therefore, their effort to communicate has less impact on the receiver. Remember, it is crucial to match the message you send to your level of feeling.

It is easy to end up with a 'YOU' statement when attempting to express anger.

It can help to think of anger as a secondary emotion, usually masking a more vulnerable feeling such as fear, insecurity, hurt, and sadness. Being angry is how we cope or deal with the primary emotion. When talking to someone close to you, it is much easier for that person to hear the immediate feelings (of hurt or fear) than to listen to the secondary emotion of anger.

For example:

Scenario (from a training video) where the mother was feeling vulnerable, neglected and insecure. Instead of expressing how she felt, she expressed herself angrily and accused him of neglecting his family.

Mother was stuck at home with a new-born baby, and father was recently promoted at work and was spending a lot of time working late. When he got home, he carried on working on his laptop. She felt ignored and neglected and that he didn't prioritise her or the baby's needs.

She prepared a special meal and has been sitting home waiting for him. He was hours late and hadn't called her. It may be very tempting to greet that individual with some form of a statement like, "I'm angry because you didn't call me, and now dinner is ruined".

Consider this alternative which expresses the primary feeling of fear: "I was scared when you were late and didn't call because I feared that you'd been in an accident".

Hear the expression of love and concern here?

In another situation where the primary feeling is being unappreciated: "I'm feeling unappreciated right now because you didn't call to let me know that you were going to be late. I wanted this evening to be special for us, and I feel like the work I put into cooking this meal has been wasted." **Hear the honesty here?**

It isn't to say that anger isn't an honest emotion - it is.

However, it takes practice and care to communicate anger in a way that doesn't cause defensiveness in another person. A great way to start is to follow the expression of anger with an 'I' statement.

For example: *"I'm angry because I feel let down."*

This is probably a better way of starting a discussion than *"I'm angry because you are late."*

The upshot is no one can argue with your feelings, or disprove them or say they didn't really happen. People can argue, however, with different interpretations of facts or behaviours.

Consider the following exchange:

What's happening now is an argument about who is disrespectful. Does this help?

Compare it to the following example: "I'm **angry because I feel disrespected when you are late. It makes me feel like spending time with me isn't important to you**".

How can anyone argue with that?

Assertiveness Techniques

Being assertive, rather than passive or aggressive, takes practice. Here are a few techniques:

1. **Broken records**

   Repeat your main point in a calm tone of voice.

   You can also rephrase the message.

   Try not to provide new information, as this allows for more discussion or argument.

   For example: "It's *just not possible for me today ... I can't do it for you today ... another day maybe, but not today."*

2. **Disagree**

   Simply say, *"I disagree"* or *"I don't agree."*

   If someone wants to keep arguing, say, *"Let us just agree to disagree."*

3. **Emphasise feelings**

   Repeat your statement of how you felt, emphasise that this is important to you.

4. **Agree ... but**

Admit the other person's point of view but repeat that yours is different.

For example: *"I see what you are saying, but it's not how I interpret things."*

5. **Dismiss detours**

Ignore attempts to side-track on to other points or issues, or point out that they are not relevant.

6. **Redefine**

Don't accept other people's negative labels.

Restate your positive interpretation of your behaviour.

7. **Question**

Don't accept vague criticism. Ask for clarification.

For example: *"In what way exactly did you think I was stupid?"*

Based on the suggested methods from the U.S. Dept of Health and Human Services (2005) with some variations as appropriate.

Guide for Working with Parents

Communicating with 'I' Statements

Explain to parents you are working with that the "I" statement is a way of saying how their actions affect you without causing conflict or escalating conflict. Rather than making judgements about the other person, you tell them how their actions affect you and why. Then you can tell them what you want or need to happen in the future and, if necessary, what you will do in response.

There are four steps to the process:

Process		Action
I feel	➡	Make an honest statement about how you are feeling
When you	➡	*Tell the person what action or behaviour of theirs has triggered your feelings*
Because	➡	Explain *what it is about their behaviour or its consequences that you don't like*
I would like it if	➡	Tell the person specifically what you want or need from them now or in the future when a similar situation arises.

'You' statements and parental conflict

When working with parents, you will find 'YOU' statements relate to some common causes of conflict. The following are examples that you may come across and need to help parents reframe:

Attention:

You never take me out anymore. You don't care about me or how I feel. You are inconsiderate; you never make time to call or text me when you are out.

Housework:

You do nothing in the house. You create more mess than the children. You are lazy. You expect me to clean up after you. You don't do your share of the housework. You are no role model; you are a bad example for the children.

Money:

You spend money selfishly and don't think about what I or the kids need. You never stick to the budget; we will never afford to go on holiday, as you just waste money.

Work:

You spend more time at work than at home. You are always working, putting work before the kids and me. You are always late getting home from work.

Sex/Intimacy:

You don't find me attractive anymore. You don't want to have sex with me anymore.

Social Media:

You spend hours on social media. You are up to no good on social media. You spend more time with people on social media with your friends than with me.

Mobile Phone:

You spend too much time on your phone, emailing, text, reading instead of paying attention to what's in front of you.

Listening:

You don't listen. You don't care what I have to say.

You and I Statement Cards

Use the cards to practice reframing 'YOU' statements. You can create cut-out cards to do direct work with parents. Identify the 'YOU' statement that parents use and then work with them to reframe it.

'YOU' Statements	'I' Statements

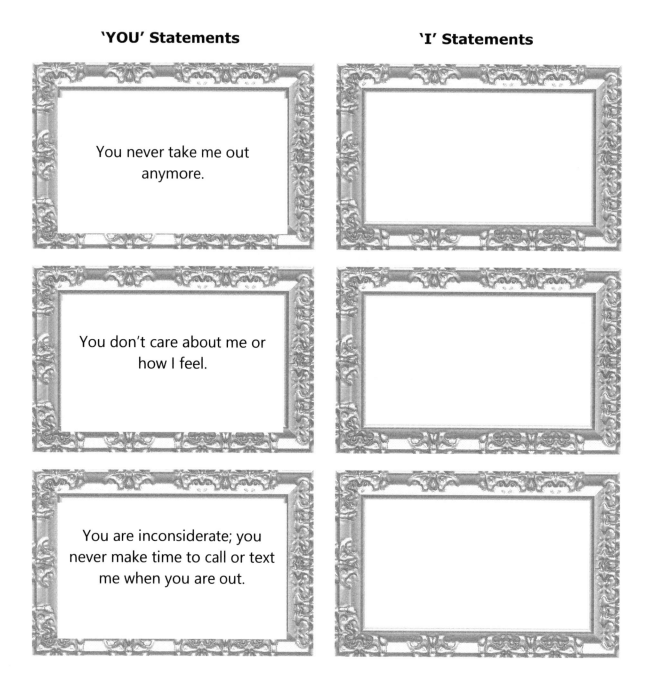

'YOU' Statements

You never take me out anymore.

You don't care about me or how I feel.

You are inconsiderate; you never make time to call or text me when you are out.

'I' Statements

'YOU' Statements	I' Statements

You do anything in the house and create more mess than the children.

You are lazy. You expect me to clean up after you.

You don't do your share of the housework.

You are no role model, you are a bad example for the children.

You' Statements   **'I' Statements**

You spend money selfishly and don't think about what me or the kids need.

You spend money selfishly and don't think about what me or the kids need.

You never stick to the budget; we will never afford to go on holiday, as you just waste money.

You spend more time at work than at home.

You' Statements   **'I' Statements**

You are always working, putting work before me and the kids

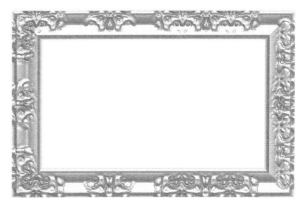

You are always late getting home from work.

You don't find me attractive anymore.

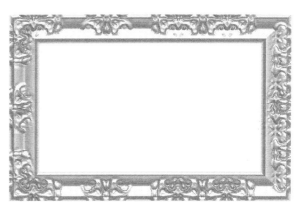

You don't want to have sex with me anymore.

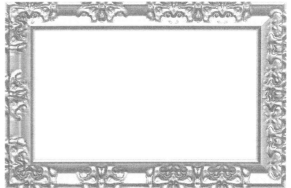

You' Statements	**'I' Statements**
You spend hours on social media. You are up to no good on social media.	
You spend more time with people on social media with your friends than with me.	
You spend too much time on your phone, emailing, text, reading instead of paying attention to what's in front of you.	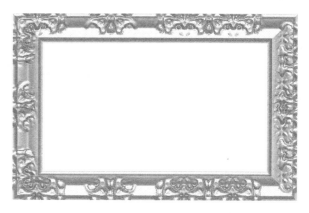
You don't listen. You don't care what I have to say.	

Constructive Versus Destructive Communication

Communicating in a constructive is not easy and can be even more difficult where there are stressors. Even when we have the best intentions, we cannot always express this positively. If this is a problem, parents will need to sharpen their communication skills to enhance their relationship quality.

Remember, outcomes for children are directly related to the quality of the parental relationship.

Positive Communication	Negative Communication
Accepting that you might disagree	Tell your partner what they should do
Asking each other's point of view	Pointing out your partner's flaws when they support your argument
Listening to the other point of view without interrupting	Withdrawing from the conversation as it's not going your way

Recognising that whilst you may not agree, your partner has a valid point

Interrupting to get your point of view across

Using insults to make your point and share your feelings

Raising your voice to make sure you get your point of view across

Choosing the right time

Using insults to make your point and share your feelings

Check out what you agree about

Having a solution in mind to the problem and don't change your mind

Show you understand the other person's point of view

Explaining how the situation is making your feel

Ending an argument both feeling that you have been heard

Ending an argument upset and angry

Considering issues from someone else's point of view

Using examples from the past to prove you are right

Allow each other the opportunity to express your views

If they have made poor choices in the past, you bring this up to prove you are right

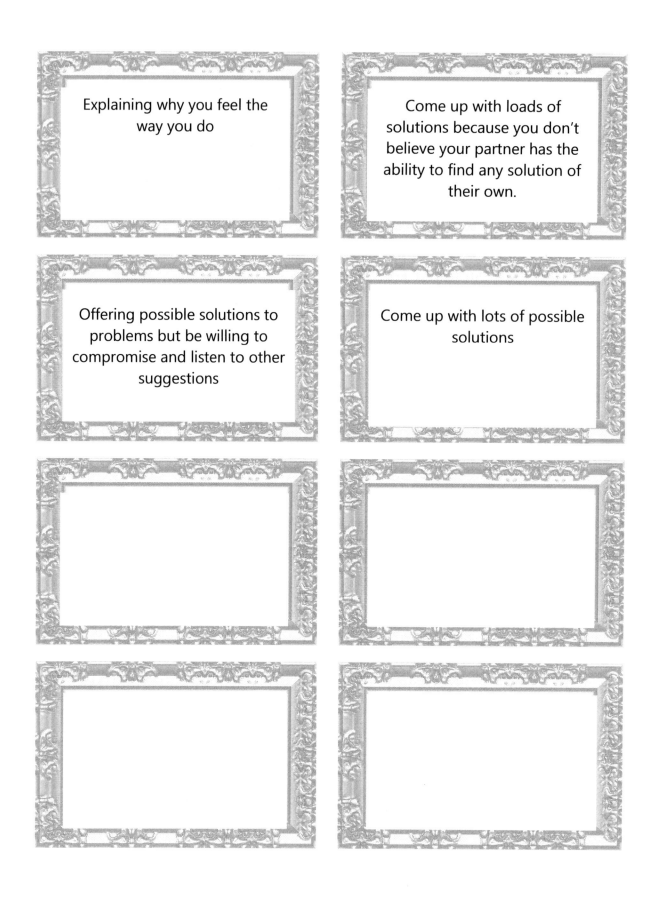

Explaining why you feel the way you do

Come up with loads of solutions because you don't believe your partner has the ability to find any solution of their own.

Offering possible solutions to problems but be willing to compromise and listen to other suggestions

Come up with lots of possible solutions

10. PART IV – Getting the Child's Voice

Parental conflict happens and affects children, whether their parents are living together or separated. When working with parents, Practitioners need to make sure they get the children's viewpoint about the conflict. Their voices must be central to the work with parents because they are the ones that will inherit the poor outcomes described in the research.

When there is a high level of conflict (frequent and intense) and animosity between parents, children are at greater risk of: -

- experiencing emotional, social, and behavioural problems

- poor educational achievement

- feeling unsafe and insecure

- damaging their relationship with their parents and others

When the parental conflict focuses on the children, it's associated with adjustment problems as children blame themselves for their parents' issues.

'Good quality parenting,' that is, parenting that provides structure, warmth, emotional support, and positive reinforcement, will reduce the conflict's negative impact. However, if the parents' parenting capacity is affected, they may not give good quality parenting.

Other factors identified as damaging how children adjust following their parents' separation include:

- the psychological adjustment of the parents after separation

- the quality and type of parenting children receives

- the relationship between parents and children

- the loss of meaningful relationships

- changes in family structures, such as parents re-partnering, and

- a reduction in financial support and resources.

Practitioners will be aware of the range of tools available to capture the child's voice. Some of these are copyrighted and need permission to replicate but have been collated and published on online.

Getting the child's voice about parental conflict requires focusing on the presenting problems. What we know from research is the types of parents' behaviours that are highly problematic are:

The types of parent behaviours that have been identified as being highly problematic are:

- asking children to carry hostile messages to the other parent

- asking children intrusive questions about the other parent

- creating a need for children to hide information

- creating a need for children to hide positive feelings for the other parent, and

- demeaning or putting down the other parent in the presence their children

Children should feel able to talk openly about their lives in both households but not feel obliged to do so. They should also feel safe when expressing their feelings, regardless of which parent is the primary carer.

As mentioned before, there are many tools and ways to work with children to capture their voices directly. How effective they are will depend on the Practitioner's skills and approach. Just remember that you have the most effective ways of engaging with children at your disposal, that is, your voice and use of self.

Children are presenting with behavioural difficulties; it is important to explore how the conflict situation affects them. Don't simply attribute a child's challenging behaviour to the child being difficult. We know from research that children can be adversely impacted in many ways:

- Withdrawn, introverted

- Anxiety, low mood and depression

- Exhibiting violent or intimidating behaviours towards others

- Showing concern and empathy for a distressed parent

- Displaying signs of emotional distress - crying a lot, being 'clingy' (younger children)

- Becoming argumentative (frequently young teenagers)

- Exhibiting disruptive behaviours – criticising parents, silences, disappearing to bedrooms, confronting parents

- Problems at school (unable concentrate, poor achievement and attendance)

- Playing one parent off against the other

- Unsettled sleep patterns and bedwetting (younger children)

List of Tools

Bin It

My Thoughts and Feelings

Using Children in Parental Conflict

All About My Day

What I Need You to Do for Me

Thoughts, Feelings, and Behavioural Response Template

10.1 Bin it (putting things the child wants to get rid of in the dustbin)

I can't recall what I was reading, but it was the concept of the 'Garbage Can Model' of decision-making. Briefly, the Model is about making decisions in an organisation when a formal decision-making process is absent.

It covers:

- Problems
- Solutions
- Contributors
- Choice opportunities

In the context of working with children and their families, the areas are explained:

1. **Problems** – arguments between parents that disrupt the family home's safety and security and harm children. The things that the parents argue about that needs attention.

2. **Solutions** – what support can be put in place to deal with the problems in the bin. Consider what the solutions are to the issues. Is there an existing method of resolving the problem?

3. **Contributors** – parents will be the main people involved as they will need to resolve the conflict. Other people who have expertise or specialism if this is necessary.

4. **Choice (Outcome)** – has things changed enough for us to take the problem out of the bin. This should be the child's choice. The Practitioner should have enough evidence to support the idea of taking the problem out of the bin.

Using the idea, you can work with the child (depending on age and understanding) by encouraging them to put the problem they are experiencing in the bin.

Explain that you will empty the bin and try to help to get the problem if possible.

You will need:

- A container with a lid
- Labels (for the child to label the bin with their name and date)
- Colour pens (or felt tips) to write with
- Square pieces of paper (post its) to write down the issue for the bin

Depending on what is happening, you might decide to open the bin and gather further information about the bin's problem. You might choose to discuss what you will be doing about the situation, go forward and reassure the child if necessary.

It might be easier if you have some cards already prepared and ask direct questions using the cards. The child is asked to put the cards in the bin if it is happening at home.

Here are some ideas that can be used to discuss what is happening in the home and what they would like to change.

10.2 My Thoughts and Feelings

In these clouds, write down all of your thoughts and feelings that they are having. They can be happy thoughts, sad thoughts, worried thoughts, excited thoughts!

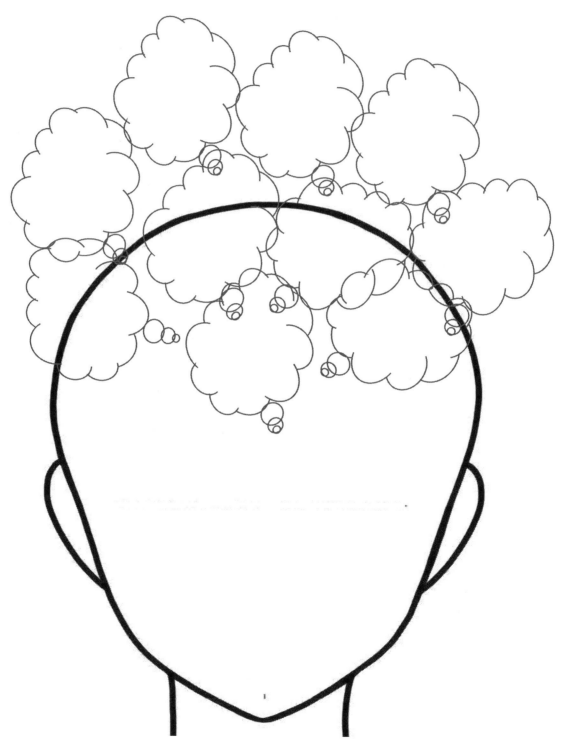

Developed by Elaine Nembhard from an unknown Author is licensed under CC BY-NC-ND

10.3 Using Children in Parental Conflict

Ensure this exercise is age-appropriate

The blanks will need to be filling in with (mum or dad) or as appropriate.
A sheet of blank cards is provided to create your own.

It upsets me, hearing my parents arguing, and shouting at each other.

Feeling Unsafe

I don't like it when my ....
gives me messages to my ....
as it usually causes upset and anger

The Messenger

I don't like it when my ....
asks me questions about my
............'s partner

The Spy

I feel like I am always in the middle, trying to keep my mum and dad from arguing– acting as the go-between

The Go-Between

It upsets me when my ....
criticises my ...., tells me something that happened and expect me to say who is right and who is wrong.

The Judge

I don't like it when my ....
tells me something and then asks me to keep it a secret from my

....

The Confidant

I sometimes think it's my fault when parents argue with each other.

I often wish they wouldn't argue as much as it makes me feel worried

I worry that my parents will split up and they will stop talking to each other.

10.4 All About My Day

The following two tools are simple and effective in capturing what is happening in the home at given times. For example, in the morning, when members of the household have to be ready for whatever they are doing during the day, whether it be work, school, nursery, or otherwise.

Completing the tool with a child will give insight into their lived experiences. You can compare the results with that of the child's parents.

If you want to know whether a child has had a good or a bad day, ask them and explore what a bad day or good day looks like. With the child, explore how they know they have had a good or a bad day.

What would it take for them to move to the other side of scale or ruler? Use the arrow to show direction to move towards, i.e., the happy face.

A child indicated things that made it a bad day; the Practitioner should respond to these appropriately.

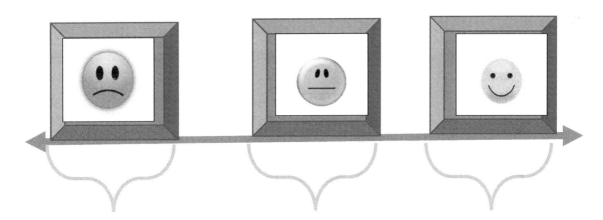

Some questions you might introduce in your discussion (must be age-appropriate):

- How were things before you had this bad day?
- What is happening now?
- What needs to change for you? What do you want to be different?
- How would things be if they were to change – what to you see happening?
- What would need to happen to make most days a good day?

10.5 What I Need You to Do for Me

The tool for working directly with the child Is on the next page. It aims to help the Practitioner find out what help the child would like and their priorities.

The Practitioner is there to help the child as well as their parent. Knowing what the child needs from you is the first step in this process. As outlined, capture the main worry in the rectangular box – this should be the most critical issue for the child. In the three smaller text boxes, make sure you work with the child to prioritise what they want to do first.

The clouds or speech boxes on the periphery are those causing hassle but not as significant as the main ones, but they still need some attention.

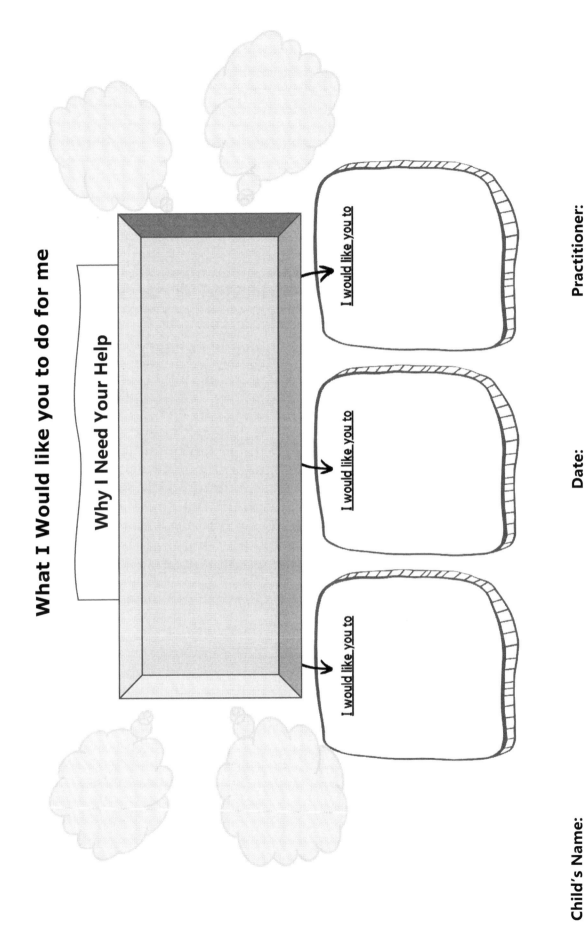

What I Would like you to do for me

Why I Need Your Help

I would like you to

I would like you to

I would like you to

Child's Name:

Date:

Practitioner:

10.6 Thoughts, Feelings, and Behavioural Response Template

Child's Version

Explain to the child that everyone has problems, some big and small. It helps you learn how your thoughts, feelings, and actions are connected to help solve the big problems.

Your parents have been arguing, and you hear them say things that make you believe they are planning to separate. Because of this thought, you start to worry. You are so worried that you feel sick just thinking about the future.

Because it's so uncomfortable, you can't concentrate at school and get angry during lessons, you feel sad and believe it's your fault.

The thought (it's my fault) led to a feeling (worry) which led to an action (misbehaving at school). What might have changed if you had a different thought?

Thoughts are words that run through your mind, the things you tell yourself about what's going on around you. There are many different thoughts you could have about a single situation.

Feelings come as a variety of things happen to you. You might feel happy, angry, sad, and lonely all in one day. Some emotions are very uncomfortable, but they are not necessarily bad. Many people have these feelings from time-to-time.

Actions are the things you do or the way you behave. Your thoughts and feelings have a notable influence on how you act. If you feel happy, you are likely to do nice things. But if you feel angry, you might not act friendly and even act mean.

What happened (in dealing with parental conflict) should be to get the child's voice about the conflict between the parents).

Then follow through on the following steps to capture the child:

- Thoughts
- Feelings and
- Actions

Summarise the steps that the Practitioner will take to support the child.

The template is on the next page:

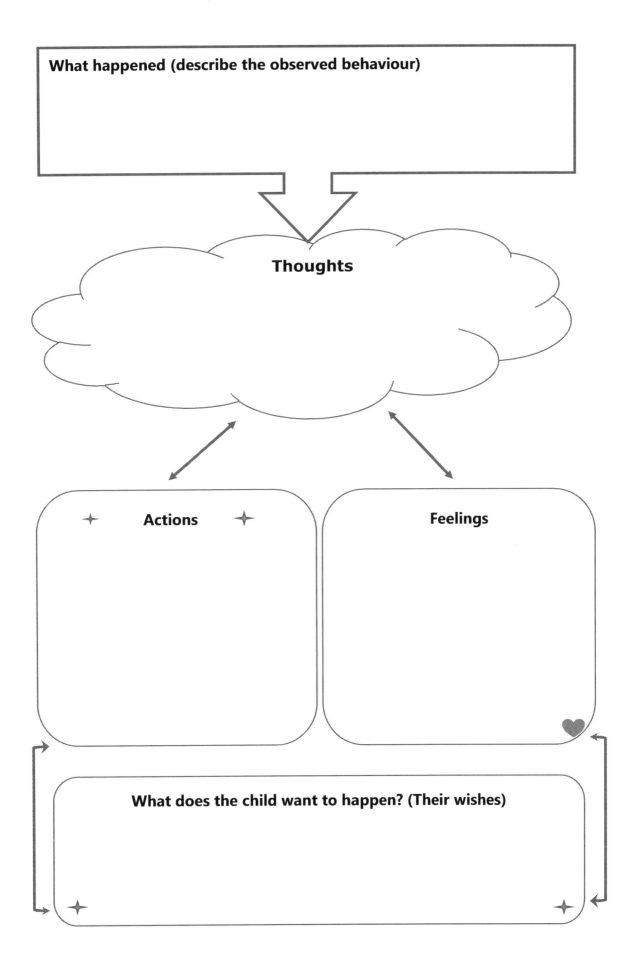

What happened (describe the observed behaviour)

Thoughts

Actions

Feelings

What does the child want to happen? (Their wishes)

Practitioners Task in Teaching Conflict Resolution

Work with parents to understand:

- what parental conflict is (difference between this and domestic abuse)
- the causes and triggers for parental conflict

- when they are in conflict how conflict escalates

- the damage that is done to children when they are exposed to parental conflict

- that children learn from their parents so they need to model positive behaviours and effectively manage or resolve their conflict

- different ways of responding to conflict and the outcomes (e.g., win-lose, win-win)

- about the readiness to change and maintain changes

- how they can deal with parental conflict through positive communication and its importance on reducing parental conflict

- where they can get support and what support is available to them

11. Part V: Practitioners' knowledge and Skills for Working With Parents and Children

This section is about bringing to attention some Practitioners' skills that are critical to working with children and their families. There is a focus on two specific areas, 'use of self' and 'professional curiosity,' while the others are mere bullet points. The ideas here are meant only as a guide to reflect on your practice.

Professional Curiosity – A Reminder for Practitioners

Over and over, **Serious Case Reviews (SCRs)** highlight the need for practitioners to be alert to the risk of **fixed thinking and perceptual bias**. Professor Eileen Munro's report (2005) drew attention to the reoccurrences in SCRs about the great lengths abusive parents will go to deceive practitioners.

Using **disguised compliance**, parents appearing to cooperate with professionals is one-way abusive parents deceive practitioners.

Professional Curiosity can help and is critical to finding out what is happening in a child's life and the risks they face at home.

Daniel Pelka SCR (2013) highlights the dangers of accepting parental versions of what is happening in the home and reminds professionals to **think the unthinkable**. Family life and contexts are constantly changing; what was true a few days or weeks ago could have changed. Remaining curious is one way to keep your judgements under critical review.

Be aware of **"confirmation bias"** sneaking into your professional practice. By this, I mean looking for evidence that confirms pre-existing views; cases should be judged objectively.

Another crucial aspect of professional curiosity is the ability to practice and maintain **"respectful uncertainty."** Lord Laming's (2003) report into the case of Victoria Climbié explained what this means. It is the capacity to explore and understand what is happening within the family rather than accepting things at face value or making assumptions.

What you can do

- Always be open-minded, keep a curious mindset, explore alternative perspectives on a situation.

- Remain child-focused and create a suitably, safe, and trusting listening environment for children and young people.

- Identifying and exploring what is and what was discussed.

- Be open to other perspectives and willing to try different responses.

- Try to build a close partnership-style relationship with the family while being constantly aware of the child's needs and how they are met.

- Use critical thinking skills sensitively and with persistence.

- Base your judgements on evidence, not optimism or assumptions.

- Be willing to research, ask questions and seek specialist advice, e.g., mental health, drugs use, or any other factor.

- Test your ability to be professionally curious safely in supervision or group supervision. Have practitioners and managers play 'devil's advocate by considering alternative actions, explanations, or hypotheses.

- Question whether you are being overly optimistic about parents' progress and ability to care for the child or their promises to engage with services.

- Learn the lessons from the SCRs by exercising appropriate professional curiosity and Investigating further.

"I did then what I knew how to do. Now that I know better, I do better."

- Maya Angelou

Use of Self

The term "use of self" is frequently used to teach in social work and practice. I have taken the term to apply to professionals from multiple disciplines working with children and their families.

It is a term that is sometimes confusing for social work students and social work discipline at large. Social workers believe they know what it means when they hear the term. When pressed, they have difficulty defining and describing the term means. Self in social work practice combines knowledge, values, and skills gained in social work education with aspects of one's self, including personality traits, belief systems, life experiences, and cultural heritage (Dewane, 2006). The use of self enables social workers to aim for authenticity and genuineness with the clients, thus honouring the values and ethics highly valued in social work practice. To explain, an example of how the use of self looks in professional practice:

When I train social workers in interviewing skills, each student covers reflecting, paraphrasing, summarising, responding, empathetic listening, questioning, and meaning. Some students will use these skill sets more effectively than others because they are demonstrated through their personality, relational skills, and individual capability.

What I have found is some students are reluctant to practice these skills in the training room through engaging in role-playing. Successful students master these skill sets because they are willing to practice using their authentic selves. Acquiring these skills allows workers to be relatable, especially with children.

Active empathetic listening (also called active or reflective listening)

Active empathetic listening (also called active listening or reflective listening) is a way of listening and responding to another person that improves mutual understanding and trust. It is an essential skill that enables the listener to accurately interpret the speaker's message and then provide a fitting response. The response is a fundamental part of the listening process. It can be critical to the success of a discussion or intervention.,

Active empathetic listening has many benefits:

- builds trust and respect,
- enables the disputants to release their emotions,
- reduces tensions,
- encourages the surfacing of information, and
- creates a safe environment that is conducive to collaborative problem solving.

Using open questions

Open-ended questions enable practitioners to ask questions that prompt the client to give more information about the problem. It allows the client to discuss critical aspects of the situation in more details.

Helps to:

- Obtain specific examples
- Expand on details and related information
- Can create an open space for further communication

Suitable for use when:

- Inviting or encouraging a client to elaborate, providing them time and space to tell their story. For example, "How have things been since my last visit?"

Reflecting back

Reflecting is the process of paraphrasing and restating both the feelings and words of the speaker. The purposes of reflecting are:

- To allow the speaker to 'hear' their thoughts and focus on what they say and feel.

- To show the speaker that you are trying to perceive the world as they see it and do your best to understand their messages.

- To encourage them to continue talking.

Reflecting does not involve asking questions, introducing a new topic or leading the conversation in another direction. Speakers are helped by reflecting as it allows them to feel understood and allows them to focus their ideas. In turn, it helps them to direct their thoughts and further encourages them to continue speaking.

Summarising

Feltham and Dryden (1993: 186) define '**summarising**' as 'accurately and succinctly reflecting the client, from time to time within and across sessions, the substance of what she has expressed'.

Summarising is a skill used to condense the main points of what the client is saying and feeling using their vocabulary or words.

Listening before questioning

Be interested, professionally curious, identify what is going on

Listen – avoid thinking about the next thing you want to say.

Avoid making assumptions – be aware of unconscious bias.

Stay away from "fix it" mode and avoid the drama triangle.

Don't take sides

Make sure you allow both parents to share their views

Empathy and questioning techniques

The use and phrasing of questions can provide a safe,

non-judgmental and empathetic environment

Starting with the words: How? Who? What? Where?

When? (and avoiding "Why?")

12. Evaluating to Evidence the Impact of Interventions

Mayday Social Work Consultancy has developed its Logic Model Creator as a process for evaluating your intervention, initiative, or project. It comes with a pre-populated performance indicator for users to select from to make the process easier.

Knowing what you want to achieve will be less daunting as we have created a database of **desired outcomes and indicators**, which you can use to **populate** your Logic Model. Our database of outcomes and indicators has been created to help you draft three types of Logic Models that respond to:

1. Reducing Parental Conflict and the Negative Impact on Children

2. Reducing Domestic Violence and Abuse and the Negative Impact on Children

3. Improving Child Protection Outcomes for Children and Reducing Child Neglect

Note: Throughout the logic model building process, we will use 'Service' to mean initiatives, interventions, projects, and programmes.

About the Logic Model?

A simple explanation is that a Logic Model tells a story using diagrams or words. What is so good about the process is that it shows the causal connection between identifying needs, what needs to be done, how this will be done, and its difference.

To explain further, here are three examples:

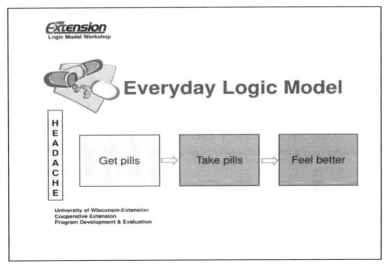

Example of the Logic Model (Fig.1)

Jones Family 'get active' plan

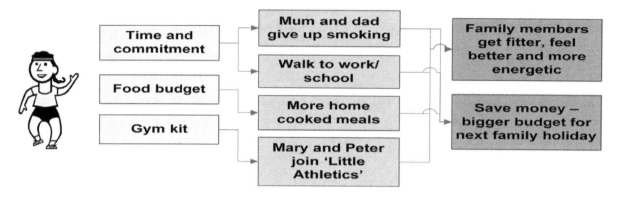

Evaluation Support Guide (Fig.2)

Parental Conflict Logic Model

Situation/Problem	Outputs		Outcomes and Impact		
	Responses	Activities	Short	Medium	Long-term
Research shows parental conflict is the primary cause of negative impact on children's outcomes, especially where it is frequent and intense.	Offer co-parenting conflict resolution workshops to couples with children (include pregnancy)	Provide practitioners with training to understand and facilitate groups or one-to-one work	Increased knowledge of the effects of parental conflict on children Learn conflict reduction techniques Learn co-parenting communication skills Identify the elements needed in a parenting plan	Develop a parenting support plan Decrease in parental arguments in front of children Increase ability to resolve parental conflict and disagreements Decrease in conflict that put children in the middle of parental relationship Increase in supportive parenting relationships	Improved child outcomes Fewer and less intense conflicts between the co-parents Improved child support maintenance payment Decrease in Court hearings due to Parental disputes and contact

Societal Impact

Better mental health for children and adults (parents and or carers)

Reduction in referrals to Statutory Children's Social Services (CSCS) where parental conflict is an issue

Reduction of the financial cost of parental conflict

Reduction in Court hearings

- NOTES -

Bibliography and Reference

Asmussen, D., Fischer, D., Drayton, E., & McBride, T. (2020). *Adverse childhood experiences What we know, what we don't know, and what should happen next.* London: Early Intervention Foundation.

Becks, J. S. (2005). *Cognitive Therapy for Challenging Problems.* New York: Beck, J. S. (2005). . New York: Guilford Press.

Department of Health. (2001). *A Framework for Assessing Children in Need and their Families.* London: Her Majesty's Stationery Office.

Gonzaga, G. C., Campos, B., & Bradbury, T. (2007). Similarity, Convergence, and Relationship Satisfaction in Dating and Married Couples. *Journal of Personality and Social Psychology* .

Gordon, H. T., & Sellers, R. (2018). *Journal of Child Psychology and Psychiatry 59:4 (2018), pp 374–402, t .* Brighton: University of Sussex.

Gordon, H., Acquah, D., Sellers, R., & Chowdry, H. (2016). *What Works to Enhance Inter-parental Relationships and Improve Outcomes for Children.* Sussex: Department for Work and Pensions.

Gottman, J., & Silver, N. (2015). *The Seven Principles for Making Marriage Work.* USA: Penguin Random House.

Graybeal, J. (2001). Strengths-based social work assessment: Transforming the dominant paradigm, Families in Society. *The Journal of Contemporary Human Services* , 82, 233-242.

Johnson, D. W. (2012). *Reaching Out: Interpersonal Effectiveness and Self-Actualization (11th ed.) .* USA: Pearson.

Karney, B., & Bradbury, T. (1995). *The longitudinal course of marital quality and stability: A review of theory, method, and research.* Karney, B., & Bradbury, T. (1995). .

Maslow, A. H. (1943). A theory of human motivation. *Psychological Review*, 370-96.

Maslow, A. H. (1987). *Motivation and personality (3rd ed.).* Delhi: Person Education.

Puiman, R. (2019). *The Mindful Guide to Conflict Resolution.* Massachusetts: Simon & Schuster.

Resnicow, K., Gobat, N., & Naar, S. (2015). Intensifying and Igniting Change Talk in Motivational Interviewing. *The European Health Psychologist*, 102.

Shaw, G. (2019). *7 Winning Conflict Resolution Techniques.* UK: Amazon.

Thomas , K. W., & Kilmann, R. H. (2008). *Thomas-Kilmann Conflict Mode Instrument Profile and Interpretive Report.* Xicom, Incorporated, a subsidiary of CPP, Inc. .

Thomas, K. W. (1977). "Toward Multidimensional Values in Teaching: The Example of Conflict Behaviours," Table 1, p. 487. *Academy of Management Review 2* , 487-490.

Ward, H., Brown, R., & Hyde-Dryden, G. (2014). *Assessing Parental Capacity to Change when Children are on the Edge of Care: an overview of current research evidence.* London: Department of Education.

Warschaw , T. A. (1980). *Winning by Negotiation.* New York: McGraw Hill.

Printed in Great Britain
by Amazon

19501150R00086